Praise for *Bad News*

"A gripping read . . . A well-structured explanation of what's wrong and how to fix it . . . [and] a convenient guide to the biggest under-reported stories and why they're important."

—*Publishers Weekly*

"A stinging indictment that gains force from [Fenton's] quarter-century of service in CBS's London bureau."

—Howard Kurtz, *The Washington Post*

"An excellent job . . . Such dedication to the news itself is infortunately rare in many recent critiques of the media . . . Fenton's earnestness has a certain nobility."

—Alexander Barnes Dryer, *The New Republic* Online

"One of the best books from inside a mainstream news organization about the shortcomings of journalism."

—Steve Weinberg, *IPI Global Journalist*

BAD NEWS

The Decline of Reporting, the Business of News, and the Danger to Us All

TOM FENTON

ReganBooks

An Imprint of HarperCollins*Publishers*

FIRST PAPERBACK EDITION PUBLISHED 2005.

Designer: Publications Development Company of Texas

The Library of Congress has cataloged the hardcover edition as follows:
Fenton, Tom, 1930–
  Bad news : the decline of reporting, the business of news,
and the danger to us all / Tom Fenton.—1st ed. x, 262 p. ; 24 cm.
0-06-079746-0
Includes bibliographical references and index.
Reporters and reporting—United States.
Press—United States.
Mass media—Unites States.
(OcoLC) ocm57896166

2005282275

ISBN 10: 0-06-085395-6 (pbk.)
ISBN 13: 978-0-06-085395-2 (pbk.)

05 06 07 08 09 PDC/RRD 10 9 8 7 6 5 4 3 2 1

To my companions on the road.

CONTENTS

PREFACE

lthough this book argues for fundamental, lasting changes in the way the news media serve the American public, it is also a snapshot of fast-changing events, as America moves from the first to the second term of the Bush administration and sinks ever deeper into the dilemma of Iraq. At the time of writing, Dan Rather has announced he will give up the anchor chair at the *CBS Evening News,* and CBS News has fired several producers and executives after the report of the independent commission charged with investigating his bungled *60 Minutes* story on the president's National Guard service found that much of the story was wrong, incomplete, or unfair. Tom Brokaw has just left the *NBC Nightly News,* and CBS is hoping to take advantage of these two departures by making changes to its flagship news show designed to pull the network out of third place. None of the networks is talking about providing more international news, more context, or serving the American public better in its time of need. Their vision is focused, as always, on the bottom line.

Writing this book has been a sobering experience, as I watch the fundamental faults of the news industry—which I dissect in the chapters that follow—become ever more pronounced. The networks are obsessed with the ratings race. Politicians and statesmen line up to appear on the ersatz news *Daily Show,* and bloggers seem to be breaking the real news. Even as the urgent problems of Iraq, Iran, North Korea, and a resurgent Russia compete for our attention, the news media fiddle while Rome burns.

—London, January 10, 2005

NOTE ON THE PAPERBACK EDITION

The death of Peter Jennings since the publication of the first edition has deprived the news industry of one of its leading in-house advocates of higher standards. Jennings believed there is a bigger market for quality foreign news, but failed to convince his corporate bosses. His voice is silent now, but his arguments echo in this book.

—London, September 10, 2005

CHAPTER ONE

THE NEWS GAP

As the monitors on the wall of the CBS News London Bureau all flashed the same mesmerizing images, I stood there spellbound. The possibilities rushed through my mind. In my four decades as a journalist and foreign correspondent, I had witnessed just about everything imaginable—from wars and revolutions to natural disasters of nearly every kind—but I had witnessed nothing like this.

When the second airplane crashed into the second tower of the World Trade Center, I knew it was not an accident, not an incredible coincidence, but the horrifying climax of a chain of events stretching back for years.

September 11, 2001, was my moment of truth. CBS News, like most of the broadcast news industry, had been sliding blithely downhill for years; on 9/11, we finally collided with a brick wall that we should have seen coming. This moment, I knew at once, represented the failure of scores of entities—but for me it was the failure of my own profession that cut deepest.

Television journalists scrambling to reach the top of their profession may have other priorities, but as an industry our most important job is to see what is coming down the road and to alert the public to the risks we find there. You won't find this part of our work in our contracts of employment. Today, you won't even find it preserved in our networks' codes of news standards. But I believe it shouldn't even have to be there. This public trust should be something every one of us feels in our guts. That's where we failed. I, and scores of my fellow American foreign correspondents, had been tracking stories about al Qaeda and its allies for more than a decade. But we rarely reported what we knew on network news—because, much of the time, our bosses didn't consider such developments newsworthy.

When Islamic militants actually *made* news abroad, of course—attacking Americans in Saudi Arabia, in Africa, in Yemen—we duly reported the tragic events. But we never fully explained who was behind them, or what compelled them to blow Americans to bits. The public saw these terrorist strikes as disconnected events that occurred without warning. But we correspondents knew otherwise. For us, 9/11 was a catastrophe waiting to happen. And September 11 was not only one of our nation's darkest days: It was also the moment that Americans realized that we were suffering from a news gap—one that had been festering for many years.

In the months that followed 9/11, CBS News and the other major American media threw all their available resources into what the White House called the "war on terror." I spent that time searching the streets and mosques of Hamburg, a haven for Muslim refugees and al Qaeda cells, to track down the story behind the story of the nineteen hijackers. I investigated an aviation school in Cologne where one of the suicide pilots took lessons. I went to Pakistan and met Taliban officials. But the networks didn't have the resources to keep this frenzy of reporting up for long, or to do the job in depth. Like NBC and

ABC, CBS News had demobilized at the end of the Cold War. We were caught without the reserves we needed, and it was largely our own fault.

Consider the success/failure record of American foreign news reporting in recent decades—a record that closely resembles our government's own performance. As a member of the American public, how many of the biggest stories were you adequately informed about ahead of time—before they burst onto your television screens? The fall of the Shah in Iran? The fall of the Soviet Union? Saddam Hussein's invasion of Kuwait? The meltdown of Afghanistan and the rise of Osama bin Laden? The catastrophe of the 9/11 attacks? None of these major events happened without a lead-up or clues to their arrival. They were years in the making. Yet to most Americans these events came from out of nowhere.

How is it that the most advanced communications society in the history of the world consistently blinds itself to the germination of epochal events abroad, even as time after time they have come home with devastating effect on our own soil?

Along with the horror and vulnerability felt by all Americans on September 11, serious journalists should also have felt that the disaster spoke directly to them. In short, they should have felt pangs of guilt. As surely as 9/11 pointed up the myriad failures of official agencies in Washington, it also revealed the abject failure of the news media.

We had failed to warn the American public of the storm clouds approaching our shores. And in failing to do so, we betrayed the trust of the public.

"The summer of 2001," says Tom Bettag, executive editor of ABC's *Nightline,* "was the lowest point in American journalism." During those months—a time when at least some members of the Bush administration were considering taking action against al Qaeda—the networks decided that the public was more interested in shark attacks than terrorist attacks. In the three months leading up to September 11, the phrase "al Qaeda" was never mentioned on any of the three evening news broadcasts—*not once*.

Instead, for example, on the eve of 9/11, here is what the *CBS Evening News* offered: a report on the sexual exploitation of young people; a story with eye-catching video on dangerous aerial stunts by military pilots; another story with in-your-face video, this one featuring a Sacramento serial killer; a piece on declining consumer spending; and two health stories—one of them about dietary supplements. In short, on the eve of our Armageddon, the evening news was a mirror image of a nation eager for titillation and fascinated with its own navel. The network's veteran anchor, Dan Rather, covered the rest of the world in a few short paragraphs, most of it trivial. Among the stories that went unmentioned: an attack by U.S. planes on Iraqi missile sites and Defense Secretary Donald Rumsfeld's ominous warning that America might have to consider a variety of methods to deal with Iraq's build up of chemical and biological weapons technology.

The content of the evening news is influenced, sometimes directly and always indirectly, by network executives. And these executives, who decide what the nation wants to know, believe that tabloid news sells. Stories that seek to explain the relevance of incremental developments in far-off countries rarely see the light of day. They get spiked by evening news producers preoccupied by ratings, because most people in our business are convinced—wrongly, I believe—that the public couldn't care less about foreign news.

No doubt, it should be the government, first and foremost, that is charged with protecting its citizens and alerting them to danger. But what happens when officials are asleep at the switch? Whose task is it, if not the news media's, to prod and goad and awaken them to their duties? Had there been a drumbeat of segments on network news showing the steadily rising Islamist threat abroad, we might be living in a different world now.

Here's a startling example of how more news stories about bin Laden and al Qaeda might have made a difference. Shortly after he arrived in America, Mohammed Atta, the man we now believe to have been the ringleader of the 9/11 attacks, went to an unsuspecting Department of Agriculture loan officer in Florida and tried to get a loan for what he described as crop dusting. He told the loan officer, one Johnell Bryant, that he wanted to finance a twin-engine, six-passenger aircraft, take out the seats, and fit it with a chemical tank that would fill every square inch except where the pilot would sit. Bryant thought the idea was impractical and rejected the application. Atta then turned his attention to an aerial photo of Washington on the wall of her office, pulled out a wad of money, and tried to buy it. He asked her to point out the White House and the Pentagon, and asked her how America would like it if another country destroyed Washington and some of the monuments in it, just as the cities in his country had been destroyed. And here's the amazing part: In the course of their conversation, Atta inquired if the loan officer had heard of an organization overseas of people disillusioned with their governments; that group, he told her, was called al Qaeda. He also mentioned the name Osama bin Laden, and promised that bin Laden would some day be known as the "world's greatest leader."

All of this took place *four months before 9/11*. But none of this rang a bell with Bryant, for al Qaeda or bin Laden were going nearly unmentioned by the mass media at the time.

After 9/11, when Bryant recognized Atta's picture, she approached the FBI. Her story matched what law enforcement

officials had heard from a captured bin Laden lieutenant—
that al Qaeda had originally planned to use small planes
packed with explosives instead of hijacked airliners.

"How could I have known?" Bryant mused to ABC News
investigative reporter Brian Ross in June 2002.[1] "Should I
have picked up the phone and called someone? You can't ask
me more often than I have asked myself that."

Johnell Bryant, of course, was a private citizen. For those
of us who are journalists, it was a different question: We
know we could have saved thousands of lives if we had done
more to bring the public's attention to the threat of an al Qaeda
attack in the years before 9/11. What we must ask now is:
Why did we fail?

Of course, some journalists were aware of the impending
threats, and tried to report them in the critical period leading
up to 9/11. But such reporters were often thwarted by their
news editors, thousands of miles away at their desks in New
York or Washington. In the summer of 2001, terrorism expert
Peter L. Bergen, the author of the in-depth al Qaeda study
Holy War, Inc.,[2] learned of a bellicose videotape made by bin
Laden that had been distributed on jihadist websites. A longtime expert of the Middle East, Bergen had been amassing intelligence that suggested a major attack was in the works,
although where and when were unclear. After obtaining a
copy of the video, Bergen passed it on to John Burns of the
New York Times, who used it as one of the centerpieces of a
story headlined "On Videotape: Bin Laden Charts a Violent
Future." The story was posted on the *Times* website two days
before 9/11. But it never ran in the paper itself.

The editor of www.nytimes.com, Bernard Gwertzman,
later called the incident "a bad screw-up."[3] He conceded that
even with all the information he had before 9/11—including
the knowledge that al Qaeda operatives were training in

American flight schools—even he had not expected a massive attack on American soil. But then piecemeal facts, buried sporadically in the back pages of even the nation's longtime newspaper of record, can never be expected to provide a complete picture of any developing situation. Without full information, you can't build up context, and without context you can't judge the importance of apparently haphazard information. Sadly, though, the *Times* didn't consider such information sufficiently interesting to share with any but the fraction of its readers who delve deeply into its online edition.

The aftermath of 9/11 saw no dramatic or serious mea culpa from the print or broadcast media—to say nothing of any concerted attempt to change their ways. There was, of course, plenty of breast-beating in the corridors of journalism. But no American network emerged publicly to say, "We failed the American people when it came to the threat of terrorism." Questioned at a news industry seminar at Stanford University on November 18, 2004, ABC News president David Weston admitted that the three big network news organizations did not ask enough questions about the Bush administration's claims that Iraq had weapons of mass destruction. "Simply put," said Weston, "we let down the American people on the weapons of mass destruction." That tells us, surely, that the people who control the airwaves simply no longer understand their roles, not to mention their duty to the public. It's hard to feel guilty for failing a task if you don't recognize it as your responsibility. At the very least, it is our job to keep our public informed of events that will affect them. We should serve as a kind of alert mechanism, an early warning system. Yet we abdicated that position in the months and years leading up to 9/11—and, in real and important ways, we have still not yet returned to the post.

There are huge gaps in the American news media's coverage of world events. We rarely send correspondents to Southeast

Asia, for example, despite the fact that an extensive network of Islamic militants there continues to plan and mount new attacks on western targets. Even less attention is paid to Africa, where American troops are engaged in a silent war to prevent that continent from becoming the next training ground and haven for Islamic terrorists. Above all, ABC News anchor Peter Jennings observes, the networks have neglected the other side of the terrorism story, as seen from the Muslim side. "What has fallen off the page," says Jennings, "has been the coverage that allows us to think actively, at least, about whether there is any way to deal with the Muslim world other than via the Bush doctrine—that is, hit them as hard as you can where you think they are, and kill them."

From anticipating the tragedies of the future, to informing public debate about potential responses, we have done far too little for far too long.

In this book, I have chosen to focus on the mainstream media—in particular the network news broadcasts. The audiences for the big three networks may be steadily declining, but polls show television is still where most Americans turn for their news.[4] In 2003, 83 percent of the American public said that they got most of their news about national and international issues from television—and that figure has remained remarkably constant for more than a decade. Only 42 percent said they got their news from newspapers, 19 percent from radio, and 15 percent from the Internet. (The survey questions usually allow more than one answer.) But here's the reality check: only 23 percent gave NBC, ABC, or CBS news the highest mark for believability. The independent media study that quoted these figures reported that the public's opinion of the media has been declining for nearly twenty years. It found that "Americans think journalists are sloppier, less professional, less moral, less caring, more biased, less honest about their mistakes and generally more harmful to democracy than they did in the 1980s." Coming from the people we are supposed to serve, that is a damning indictment.

Yet the public's verdict has had little impact on the mindset of media executives. You won't see any media heads roll for neglecting to give the public enough news, or better and timelier information on the state of the world. Heads roll for other reasons, of course—on television, for low ratings; on network news, for not garnering maximal advertising revenue, not eking out the fullest profit for the parent corporation.

In the print media, heads frequently roll for individual lapses in probity—from plagiarism to faking of sources or evidence. The fabrications of *New York Times* reporter Jayson Blair were so egregious that they led to the resignation of the newspaper's two top editors, Howell Raines and Gerald Boyd. But publications naturally treat such incidents as wild aberrations. Once they've persuaded themselves that they've isolated and excised the anomaly, all is well: the flaws cannot therefore be systemic. The same thing happens when newspapers print corrections of factual errors. The implication is that everything else in the paper is true. The real questions, of course—the ones that go to the heart of the system—never get asked. Do media organs give us enough of the truth (otherwise known as news), or do they consistently miss large, crucial, chunks of it? Do they even know what the real news is?

In mid-2004, the *New York Times* and the *Washington Post* announced publicly that they had failed to scrutinize the Bush administration's given reasons for invading Iraq sufficiently in advance of the war. The *Times* printed an apology on May 26, admitting that it had misled its readers on the issue of weapons of mass destruction. "Editors at several levels who should have been challenging reporters and pressing for more skepticism were perhaps too intent on rushing scoops into the paper," the extraordinary statement read. "Accounts of Iraqi defectors were not always weighed against their strong desire to have Saddam Hussein ousted. Articles based on dire claims about Iraq tended to get prominent display, while follow-up articles that called the original ones into question were sometimes buried. In some cases, there was no follow-up at all." Even leaving aside whatever political agenda such an admission may imply, *Times* readers could be forgiven for wondering: Was this confessed oversight a unique situation? What else had the paper missed, and for how long?

Almost simultaneous to the admission, Defense Secretary Donald Rumsfeld declared smugly at a news conference that it was the military, not the media, who had uncovered the abuse of Iraqi detainees at Abu Ghraib prison. After the story became a global scandal, the *Columbia Journalism Review* took up the matter, asking, "Why did it take so long for the media to break the story of prisoner abuse at Abu Ghraib?" The *Review* pointed out that the watchdog organizations Amnesty International and Human Rights Watch had been complaining of persistent prisoner abuse in Afghanistan and Guantanamo Bay for two years. The U.S. military in Iraq had itself released information of an ongoing internal investigation months before, in January 2004. At the time, some papers had run short items reporting the press release—once again, in their inside pages. The story would have died there if the CBS News program *60 Minutes II*, more than three months later, had not broadcast the infamous pictures that set off a firestorm of protest around the world. A "high level source" had called CBS News in January and said he had seen the photographs and was so shocked by them that he "had to tell someone." The source felt the American public should see them. *60 Minutes II* spent two months tracking down the pictures and verifying their authenticity—and then delayed broadcasting the pictures for two weeks at the request of the Pentagon, while arrangements were made for someone from the military to respond on the program.

Don't get me wrong. I am not writing this book to knock my profession, or to denigrate the company that has given me so many happy years on the front row of world events. I am writing this because we can—and we must—do a lot better. After almost four decades as a foreign correspondent, covering Europe, the Middle East, the Indian subcontinent, Central Asia, and bits of Africa, I am now in a position to give my own views on what we do and how we do it. I would like to give back something to my profession—the sense of responsibility to the public that we seem to have forgotten.

Throughout my career, I have prided myself on staying ahead of the curve. A sense of duty and urgency motivated and drove me—to find out what was coming down the road, or lurking behind the next corner, and to report it to the American public. That was my job, my fun, my life—until the mega-corporations that have taken over the major American television news companies squeezed the life out of foreign news reporting.

In the decade leading up to 9/11, I had been beaten down by the corporate bean counters. I had seen so many of my stories rejected, so many proposed trips in search of news turned down by executives more interested in furthering their careers by coming in under budget than in breaking real news, that I had almost given up. You can be rejected only so many times before you stop trying, before you stop informing the public fully. In my view, corporate greed and indifference have all but killed the kind of newsgathering ethos that produces results.

And there is another problem, more insidious because the public isn't aware of it. The London Bureau of CBS News, where I have spent more than a quarter century, doesn't do much reporting any more. What it does is called *packaging*. We take in pictures shot by people we do not know, and wrap them in facts gathered by anonymous employees in news agencies owned by others. Call it the news media's version of outsourcing. All the television networks now do most of their "reporting" this way, to save money on old-fashioned shoe-leather reporting by full-time correspondents. And as a result, the networks can no longer vouch for much of the foreign news they put on the air. Just as Dan Rather did so disastrously with those dodgy Bush memos that hastened the end of his career as anchor of the *Evening News,* they take it on trust. Don't shoot it, don't report it—just wrap it up and slap the CBS eye on it. And hope you won't notice the difference.

The dangerous news gap in America should not be a partisan matter. At its heart, it has little or nothing to do with the politics of left and right. Nor should debates over patriotism or defeatism confuse the issue. At the same time when the media was overlooking the Abu Ghraib story, it was also persistently ignoring the real positive developments in Iraq: the opening of schools and shops, the revival of commerce and the return of normal life in many cities. But when the *New York Times* finally got wind of the prisoner abuse story, it ran endless front-page blockbusters on the topic, as if in atonement for its initial apathy. Then the backlash set in: the Rush Limbaughs and Fox News hosts smelled unpatriotic leftism in the relentless coverage and moved in for the kill.

Don't misunderstand me: There's no doubt that the Abu Ghraib story played well to the liberal bias of the *Times* when the paper finally woke up. There's no question that political biases do exist among editors, producers, and reporters. They naturally affect the choice and spin of stories, as my former CBS News colleague Bernard Goldberg has noted.[5] After all, there have been very few stories on the intimidation and torture perpetrated by al Qaeda or the Iraqi resistance on their own people.

But partisan sniping should not distract from the greater problem. Too much is at stake. There is a different and scarier story than political bias in the media. It is a deep-rooted repetitive pattern on the part of an industry that's not up to the task. David Javerbaum, the head writer for *The Daily Show*—the nightly spoof of network news, which now attracts more 18- to 34-year-old viewers than the real thing—put it this way: "I think the problem of bias—liberal/conservative bias—is a red herring," he says. "The real bias is toward laziness, toward entertainment, toward confrontation, toward that which will drive the ratings. The real story is this incredible laziness. It seems like the whole institution has lost its way."[6]

Some people in our business think the news coverage we offer the public is so thin that they consider it a waste of time to watch the traditional evening news shows. Don Hewitt, the CBS News executive who invented the evening news format before going on to create *60 Minutes,* the most successful news magazine in the history of television, recently admitted to me that *even he* no longer bothers to watch the *CBS Evening News.* "Can't watch it," he told me. "First of all, all day long I'm hearing Fox [and] CNN. There was a time when you had to wait until you got home at night to watch either Walter Cronkite or Huntley-Brinkley to find out what happened today. [Now] there is not a soul in London, New York, Paris, who does not know what happened today, before seven o'clock at night. It's on their car radio. It's on all-news television. . . .

"In a universe that has all-night and all-day news, you can't give them sixteen, seventeen minutes of news a night and say that's anything other than just wallpaper. That's all the hell it is."

In a survey conducted after 9/11, editors from newspapers with circulations over 100,000 were asked to rate foreign news coverage in America; most judged it only fair or poor. Martin Baron, the editor of the *Boston Globe,* admitted post-9/11 that "we [journalists] do bear some responsibility for American ignorance" on world affairs. Marvin Kalb, once a CBS and NBC correspondent and now an academic at Harvard, said that "the news industry has not been glowingly successful in coverage in the war on terror." Edward Seaton, a former president of the American Society of Newspaper Editors, put it more bluntly: "While we can debate whether [our] failure played a role in our national preparedness, there is no question that we failed our readers."

These days, more than ever before, the news media have come under constant and minute public scrutiny for their shortcomings. When *The New Yorker*'s media reporter Ken Auletta spent time at the White House for an inside look at the Bush administration and the press, he concluded "that senior staff members there saw the news media as just another special interest group whose agenda was making money, not serving the public." But this was no mere snipe at the Bush administration's habit of holding the press at bay: Increasingly, surveys suggest that the public agrees.

There is certainly a great deal of agonized self-examination in the organized news business. From debates on C-Span to forums at Harvard's Kennedy School for Government and any number of think tanks in Washington and around the country, you can watch endlessly as powerful media figures debate their role, deny their political biases, and avow their consummate sense of responsibility. Cable TV programmers always find a place for this kind of self-important theater of hot air and posturing. Yet all that babble of debate and scrutiny manages to miss the point, or so it seems. Witness the excuses offered for muffing the Abu Ghraib story: the Bush administration's skill at news management, the Pentagon's penchant for covering up the less attractive side of the American occupation of Iraq, the difficulties and danger in getting at the facts in Baghdad—ad hoc reasons with finite implications. As usual, the media never came close to conceding the systemic flaws that actually underlie all such problems. Loren Jenkins, foreign editor for National Public Radio, has been among those lamenting the Bush administration's skill at news management. "I have never seen greater news management in thirty-plus years in this business," he says. But he admits that such stonewalling isn't supposed to stop the inquisitive journalist: "That's what the Fourth Estate is all about—poking holes in news management."[7]

Even more damning was this recent analysis in the *National Journal* by Vaughn Ververs:

> Many point to the uber-patriotism they say was prevalent in the wake of Sept. 11 as an excuse for the media's lack of scrutiny of the case for war. Others complain about the selective, if not inaccurate, information given to the press by the administration.
>
> The result has been an avalanche of negative coverage for the administration and, in many cases, an easy ride for the

Democratic ticket. . . . Doom and gloom coverage throughout the press raised many a doubt about the handover of
power to an interim Iraqi government.

From Iraq to the economy, Bush was buffeted by bad
news—and worse headlines. None of the news was fabri-
cated or made up in any way. These weren't hit pieces on the
president. But the way in which they were played signaled
that the media would give the administration no more free
passes. And that's just where our sympathy for the press
ends. Rather than focus on the skeptical coverage of late,
more folks should be asking why? Why was the coverage in
the run-up to the war less questioning and probing? Why
would any administration be given any free passes? And,
most importantly, why blame those in power for the media's
shortcomings?[8]

The answer, surely, is that the industry has slipped so far that
it has lost the ability even to critique itself.

This kind of thing happens, from time to time, to almost
every industry. It happened to Detroit in the 1970s, and to
Wall Street during the tech boom of the late 1990s. In this
case, though, we are at war; the stakes are greater than simply
an economic downturn; they are a matter of life and death.

In fact, despite all the discussion within my profession
about the content of mainstream news media and the proliferation of news purveyors, the amount of hard news the public
receives has not really increased. Much of the noise, in recent
years, has focused on the political partisanship of journalists.
The ratings success of the Fox News Channel and the proliferation of radio talk shows of the left and right, from Rush
Limbaugh to the liberal radio network Air America, might

suggest that Americans get more news than ever. Sadly, much of this extra media output is spent on commentary and political sniping, rather than broader coverage of foreign events, or on fresh investigative reporting, or on telling Americans more about what's actually happening in the wider world. Instead, the public gets an outpouring of brazen hostility and name calling, from personalities and pundits all too eager to bludgeon home their points.

Talk radio and television shows may be popular, exciting, and sometimes wickedly funny. But they shouldn't be confused with news.

In the two decades before September 11, American newspaper editors and television executives reduced their coverage of foreign news by 70 to 80 percent. Those looking for more in-depth coverage did have other options in cable TV and the Internet, but the cable news networks rely more on commentary than coverage, and the online world especially can be hard to navigate, and often even harder to trust. Mainstream foreign reporting did see a brief renaissance after bin Laden's 9/11 wake-up call, but it did not last long. There was no mass reopening of foreign bureaus, no large-scale hiring of skilled journalists. Within months, we were back to business as usual.

CBS's Dan Rather believes he missed an opportunity after 9/11 to convince his bosses to reverse years of decline and cost cutting. "In looking back," he told me recently, "we may have missed an opportunity to go at that time with our boldest, most aggressive, most integrity-filled pitch, for rebuilding our international coverage in a significantly dramatic new way. And I include myself in that—we may not have made the case strong enough, quick enough, in the wake of 9/11. Because I remember that very quickly after 9/11, it was, *What do you need? Bring it to us and we'll try to arrange it.*"

Nowadays, any journalist recently returned from Iraq or Afghanistan or the Middle East has the same experience: at a hometown bar or dinner party or in the office, we're confronted by friends who ask, "What's really going on over there?"

If our industry were doing its job, no one would have to ask.

Americans can sense that they're underinformed. They know that they don't know enough. A pervasive feeling has haunted many Americans since the attacks of September 11— a fear that all manner of shadowy forces and strategies are at play beyond their ken, and that we the people are powerless to shape or even react to them—in large part because our access to information is so flawed. If their news media could ignore or miss so big a story as the coming attacks on the World Trade Center and the Pentagon, what else have they missed and what are they missing today?

It doesn't help matters when the industry indulges in cheap agonizing over its predicament—while remaining clueless about self-diagnosis and real reform. Why else would a nakedly polemical vehicle such as Michael Moore's *Fahrenheit 9/11* do so well, if not because Americans increasingly feel they must look beyond the established sources for their information?

Most of the world gets international news that differs significantly from American news or from the American point of view. Much of this is dismissed stateside as mere anti-Americanism, but it is also true that America's actual role in the world is more visible the further one gets from America's shores. Foreigners are regularly exposed to some of the more awkward facts about U.S. policy—facts that simply don't surface in our mainstream news media.

Most Americans, for example, had no idea that during the 1990s U.S. agents were working with the Taliban in Afghanistan with a view to establishing a "friendly" regime that would allow western oil companies to build a pipeline across their country. I first stumbled on that story in neighboring Turkmenistan in 1995, but could never get it on the air; CBS didn't think it was news. Perhaps it wasn't front-page material at the time, but a proper investigative operation would have grabbed at the chance to show the American government cozying up to wild-eyed fundamentalists, because of the potentially unpredictable consequences. Like America's earlier clandestine support for bin Laden and his anti-Soviet "freedom fighters" in Afghanistan, it was another case of America's chickens coming home to roost. Although the story eventually became widely known in the Middle East, it wasn't until Michael Moore's film that most of the American public knew anything of these inconvenient facts. Facts like these may each only represent small parts of the total picture, but they add up. Eventually, they may or may not mean anything important in the larger picture, but how can Americans judge if they don't know in the first place? Any foreign correspondent with a modicum of experience will tell you of such facts by the dozen floating around that never reach the American public.

Donatella Lorch, former foreign correspondent for the *New York Times, Newsweek,* and NBC News and now the director of the Knight International Press Fellowship in Washington, reports that many of her colleagues have fled from the large news organizations with a sense of failure. "I know there are many TV reporters who feel frustrated by the inability to get news out and on the air," she says. "It is terribly frustrating when you can't persuade your executive producers that what's happening in Afghanistan is more worthy of airtime than Laci Peterson or Michael Jackson."

The gatekeepers of the news—the executives, editors, and producers who decide what information will make it to the public—will tell you that the the average reader simply cannot absorb that much hard news, especially about events abroad. On one level, they're merely restating the problem: Americans are too broadly underinformed to digest nuggets of information that seem to contradict what they know of the world. Yet whose fault is that, and whose responsibility is it to correct? Instead, news channels prefer to feed Americans a constant stream of simplified information, all of which fits what they already know. That way they don't have to devote more air time or newsprint space to explanations or further investigations.

Yet it's precisely through the information that gets left behind—through those awkward and contrary tidbits of news that litter the cutting-room floor—that we get breakthroughs to the truth. Take two recent books penned by lone investigators who uncovered hidden conspiracies by following up on overlooked loose ends. When veteran CNN producer Steven Emerson accompanied an Arabic-speaking friend to a mosque in Oklahoma soon after the first World Trade Center bombing, the conversations he heard at the mosque—and the contacts he made in the wake of the visit—astonished him. Leaving his job at CNN to go freelance, he devoted himself throughout the 1990s to tracking down the network of Islamic charities connected to Hezbollah, Islamic Jihad, and al Qaeda. He warned authorities and anyone willing to listen of a likely second attempt on the World Trade Center. Predictably, nobody listened—until after September 11. Ultimately, his information helped unravel extremist charities operating in the United

States; eventually he was called to testify before the Senate. The whole frustrating and cautionary story is related in his book *American Jihad.*

Similarly, Peter Lance, a veteran television and print journalist with five Emmy Awards, decided after 9/11 to investigate the history of terror networks in New York City. He stumbled across critical information about Ramzi Yousef, the mastermind behind the first World Trade Center bombing. In his book *1000 Years for Revenge,* Lance reveals how the FBI downplayed the full implications of that first terrorist attack, thereby—according to Lance—allowing the 9/11 plotters to keep on working unmolested. The connections Lance documents were overlooked by both the authorities and the media.

Each of these journalists worked outside the organized news media. And each began by pursuing the signals given out by anomalous loose ends overlooked in their news zone—precisely the kind of news that mainstream media don't notice or pursue. Were it not for their lone determination, neither the public nor the authorities would know of the crucial material they have uncovered. Nor, without them, would we know how badly our public servants have performed. Why did they succeed where the entire machinery of the news industry failed?

As we will see, the standards in the news industry have declined, from multiple causes and in many ways. There are many excuses, some seemingly reasonable—yet no longer acceptable. Clearly, the media executives who control the news do not believe it falls to them to undertake such complex long-term investigations as these authors did. That kind of work is expensive, after all, and it can lead to complex stories that may be hard for the public to follow. Much easier to feed them brain candy.

But the barbarians are inside our gates. And with the threats to our security now apparent as never before, nothing can trump hard information about our security—not even weight loss programs, or the sex lives of politicians. *Give the public what they want* is no longer good enough. America has awakened to the dangers of junk food. It's time to launch the fight against junk news.

CHAPTER TWO

WARTIME DUTIES

WHAT IS AT STAKE, AND WHAT IS OUR ROLE?

A rguably, the United States now lives under greater threat than at any time since Pearl Harbor. We are a country, a people, at war—a war in which the enemy has declared its intention to harm the homeland. Our cities live in the daily shadow of a dirty bomb attack. Every hour casts new doubts on the safety of our water supplies, nuclear power stations, ports, monuments, tunnels, bridges, and population centers. Two months after 9/11, Osama bin Laden told a Pakistani journalist that he had chemical and nuclear weapons and was prepared to use them in self defense.[1] And after the fall of Kabul in 2002, foreign correspondents found documents in safe houses and training camps that indicated that al Qaeda was working on bioweapons for use against the United States. We might suddenly need to contend with emptying cities, vast refugee crises, epidemics nationwide, and a collapsed economy. I am not conjuring up unlikely nightmares: The enemy evidently plots such scenarios, and our government has openly told us about it.

And it has just begun to dawn on us that our country remains ill-equipped to handle any of these challenges. One of the unreported stories of the past few decades is the neglect of America's public health services. The preventive services that should make up our country's first line of defense against disease have deteriorated to the point where, in some respects, we are essentially defenseless.

Does anyone think the news media have fully adapted to this new reality? You could argue in defense of journalism that it takes time to adapt to such radical change, that there's a lot of ground to make up. You might equally argue that the news media should be out in front leading the charge, priming the public.

Perhaps the most charitable way to understand why our industry is failing us so badly is to understand the difference between the role of news in peacetime and in wartime. The rise of news media ineptitude broadly parallels the post-Cold War 1990s decade of complacency during a time of apparent peace. (I say "apparent" because in truth the decade was anything but peaceful, and our complacency had more to do with greed and self-obsession than with any real response to outside realities.) We are now living in a time of war, and the news media must bestir itself radically out of that decade's bad habits. Our industry has fallen into appalling stagnation, at a time when we need it to be most alert and competent. Beyond the firefight over patriotic or unpatriotic reporting, no one has yet debated the different roles that peace and war impose on national news media.

Our paramount function, of course, is to warn the public. Veteran correspondents who remember the changes from World War II onward will tell you that our wartime job has become more and more complex with the new challenges of each era. It used to be that we simply had to warn against the conventional enemy out there. The McCarthy era focused on the Congressional witch hunt for the hidden enemy within (the

1950s' version of al Qaeda sympathizers on American shores). The Vietnam era added another enemy: the obfuscations and incompetence of our own government. These days, the correspondent must counter a new enemy for the public's sake: the incompetence of our own news media industry, the under funding, the dumbing down and pandering to ratings by our bosses. Until the 1990s, correspondents simply didn't face the kind of know-nothing resistance to foreign affairs reporting that has since come to pose a new threat to the public.

The modern role of news in wartime has its roots in World War II, when American foreign correspondents became part of the war effort, wearing uniforms as they covered the military units to which they were assigned. Edward R. Murrow's rooftop broadcasts from London for CBS News during the blitz went beyond great reporting. They served as propaganda designed to bring home to Americans the reality of a war that could not be won without the United States. Once America entered the war, few correspondents questioned the decisions of their leaders. None doubted the justness of that war, nor the need to keep the public informed of world affairs and alert to dangers from abroad. At that time, America's leaders had so successfully united the country that the news media never questioned the war itself or the actions of our leaders in waging it.

The Korean War added another dimension to the job of the news with the advent of television, but did not fundamentally alter its role. Newspapers and radio were still the main source of news, but CBS television provoked controversy in August 1950 by reporting an infantry landing while it was under way—a security breach that was a harbinger of future tensions between those who waged war and those who covered it.

That tension came to a head a decade and a half later, when America waded into the jungle of Vietnam. An initially unquestioning press gradually began to see the gap between their government's upbeat rhetoric and the downbeat reality they saw on the battlefield. It was perhaps the first American example of patriotism in wartime being founded on skepticism, on criticism of the war by the press. There seemed to be a yawning divide between the interests of the public and the interests of the government. As in any true democracy, the news media discovered that its patriotism lay in serving the public first. When CBS News anchor Walter Cronkite, initially a supporter of the war, proposed an "honorable" withdrawal from Vietnam, President Lyndon Johnson knew he had lost the support of his country.

The coverage of America's wars after that disillusionment remained largely adversarial. The military mistrusted the correspondents, and the correspondents mistrusted the military. Commercial television cameras were completely shut out of the American invasion of Grenada in 1983. In the first Gulf War, the media could not be banned, but military brass kept reporters away from the action and fed the press pool a steady diet of briefings illustrated with videos of bull's-eyes against Iraqi bunkers.

In the second Gulf War, both the military and the media came full circle. The military embraced the media, embedding correspondents and camera teams with combat units, and reaped a harvest of gung-ho reports from the battlefield. In the process, the media largely forgot their role as critical observers. They became part of the Pentagon's battle plan. That lasted until the turbulent postwar insurrection, when all the comparisons to Vietnam, initially dismissed as liberal media bias, began to look justified. By the time of President Bush's successful campaign for reelection, the government's credibility gap had risen to Vietnam proportions—but for the first time, as a result of inadequate resources and incompetent coverage, the news media's credibility gap was even worse.

Of course, the war that got the most sustained coverage in the years since World War II was not a war at all—it was a gargantuan standoff between civilizations, each of which had the nuclear capacity to destroy each other. The Cold War kept both the military and the media on their toes; those decades supplied foreign correspondents with their daily bread and butter, with a sense of mission and the respect of their bosses. The journalists of those years kept the public apprised of the shifting tensions between the powers, and the public placed great importance on their function. As ABC News anchor Peter Jennings points out, "The mere suggestion that the Soviets were up to something somewhere meant that your superiors immediately put you on a plane to cover it, whatever it was." In those years, foreign news was real news; the Cold War encouraged the big media organizations to maintain worldwide networks of bureaus and correspondents.

It was the heyday of foreign correspondence, but it didn't last.

After the Cold War ended and the Soviets retreated, the country as a whole relaxed its vigilance. The ensuing years saw a massive and damaging cutback in military and intelligence funding, to the extent that—to our great expense, as we all know—the intelligence services utterly lost their sense of mission. They stood down; few among them saw 9/11 coming, despite repeated warnings and indicators, and those who did discovered that their White House bosses were happy to ignore them.

Much the same happened to America's news organizations: They cut back on foreign staffs and international news gathering at precisely the moment the world was becoming less predictable and more dangerous. Foreign correspondents like myself came to be regarded as alarmists, waving our arms from remote places like Rwanda or Yugoslavia, trying in vain to attract attention. In January 1993, I spent the better part of a week in Kosovo investigating Serbian police brutality and witnessing the Muslim majority's fears that the Serbs planned a campaign of ethnic cleansing. Centuries-old Balkan hatreds, seething beneath the surface, were threatening to erupt again. I stood on a freezing hilltop above Pristina, the capital of Kosovo, to wrap up my piece on camera, hoping that my words would have an impact.

What was it that had me so concerned? Well, a potential conflict at the heart of Europe, the first since World War II, could definitely affect American vital interests. Anyone with the slightest knowledge of European history knew that Balkan wars inevitably pulled in major powers; most notoriously, it was trouble in the Balkans that had triggered World War I. In this latest version, after Germany provocatively recognized the independence of Croatia from Yugoslavia, Russia immediately took the Serbian side in a pan-Slavic gesture of solidarity. The signposts all pointed to renewed disaster. Americans needed to know that, as had happened so often in the past, they might have to get involved again. Here's what I reported:

> If the situation here explodes, the assumption is that neighboring countries will be sucked into the conflict, including perhaps Greece and Turkey, both NATO members. The fear in Western capitals is that this tiny republic could be the spark for a wider war in the Balkans.
>
> —Tom Fenton, CBS News, Pristina.

I could have saved my breath. Without batting an eye, Dan Rather turned blithely to the next item on the *Evening News:* "Coming up next, Eye on America. Tonight, a first-of-a-kind apartment building. The rent includes homework."

We lived in a country at peace for the first time in decades—or so it seemed. Who cared about far-off places with obscure problems? Much of Europe, for one: Within a few years, the Balkan conflict had so widened that it sucked all of NATO—including the United States—into its maw.

On the home front, however, Americans viewed the post-Cold War years as a time to reap the so-called "peace dividend." The post-Soviet years coincided with the Clinton-Gore era, in which the president's sex life and domestic celebrity gossip in general became accepted as the legitimate currency of headlines. In the new media environment of cable, satellite, and the Internet, gossip and entertainment journalism expanded massively as a revenue-earning genre—a situation that lasted into the Afghan and Iraqi invasions, when editors had to send gossip reporters to war zones for lack of qualified personnel.

In the wake of bin Laden's ascendance, the social tenor of that low delusional decade has already been forgotten. It was a time when only social misfits or policy wonks brought up nasty foreign news issues at dinner parties; instead, Americans considered it *de rigeur* to chatter about Donald Trump's girlfriends or Joey Buttafuoco's shenanigans. The winning of the Cold War generated a kind of unthinking Americo-centric cultural triumphalism: if this was the best political-economic system in the world, then Americana and pop culture—in short, we ourselves—deserved to be the center of the news universe. And, like everyone else, the news bosses felt they had a right to relax too, to make money while ignoring the woes of the outside world.

Put aside, for a moment, the fact that vigilance about trouble abroad is a news organization's responsibility. The real problem with the relaxed posture of the media during the 1990s is that neither the country nor the world was really at peace. The post-Soviet years ushered in a period of global instability that Cold War polarities had hitherto suppressed. Remember the Gulf War, Somalia, the Balkans war, not to mention vicious little conflicts in the old Soviet space such as Nagorno-Karabagh and Chechnya?

Democracy itself almost crumbled in Russia under the drunken incompetence of President Boris Yeltsin, whose reelection the Clinton White House virtually planned and funded. President Clinton regarded Yeltsin as an "an Irish poet [who] sees politics as a novel that he's writing or a symphony that he's composing,"[2] and supported him to the bitter end—even when Yeltsin dissolved the Congress of People's Deputies in 1993 and adopted a new constitution granting himself almost dictatorial powers. Later, in 1996, the Clinton administration deployed IMF loans in such a way as to help Yeltsin win reelection, and then portrayed his victory as a triumph of democracy—playing first and foremost, as usual, to his audiences at home. While the Yeltsinites were losing one war in Chechnya and needed to stoke a second in order to remain relevant, Mafia interests bought up much of Russian industry and influenced Kremlin policies. The Russian people lapsed into poverty and grew heartily sick of "democracy," which predisposed them to accept the near-dictatorship of the nation's current president, Vladimir Putin. All the while, the Clinton White House ignored all evidence that Russia was on the brink at home, and fomenting trouble on its periphery. As long as the United States avoided full engagement with trouble abroad, it would all somehow go away.

But if America managed to maintain peace with a corrupt Russian leader, we were effectively at war in other parts of the world. Only it didn't suit our profit-happy media bosses or our politicians to see things that way. Americans suffered direct attacks repeatedly: in the first World Trade Center bombing in New York in 1993; at an Air Force apartment complex in Saudi Arabia in 1996; in Africa against two of our embassies in 1998; and against the *U.S.S. Cole* in Yemen in 2000. To which the Clinton administration responded by ineffectually lobbing cruise missiles against a pharmaceutical factory in the Sudan[3] and a training camp in Afghanistan. The world was at war, and we were in increasing peril, but our political leaders chose not to notice.

And the news media followed suit. Sure, they reported all those disasters, but they never consistently connected the dots. No rising crescendo of alarm reached the public's ears. The gatekeepers of national news turned down one foreign story after another because "foreign news doesn't sell." (To which the obvious answer, *It won't sell until you "sell" it,* was rarely heeded.) It was a vicious circle. The less we told the public about the turbulent events beyond our shores, the less interest Americans were likely to develop in foreign news. Such events seemed to Americans ever more isolated and disconnected from their comfortable existence.

Correspondents who risked their lives in far-off trouble spots found that executives back home valued their efforts minimally. What a difference from Cold War days! Almost overnight, it seemed, top news executives in New York suddenly forgot how to judge or value important news. In the blink of an eye, they lost the sense of mission to their fellow citizens that had driven them for so many years. If the American public "wanted" pap, by golly they were going to get it, by the bucketful—and damn the consequences.

One of my CBS News colleagues remembers covering the aftermath of a mortar attack on a primary school in Sarajevo in the early 1990s, when the war still raged with intensity. The attack killed four or five children and injured a dozen, including their teacher. The video that cameraman Nick Turner shot was strong and moving. Correspondent Barry Petersen wrote a beautifully crafted script. They carefully edited the piece to avoid the most gruesome pictures and fed it by satellite to New York. The next morning, when the team woke up and read the "logs" from New York listing the stories that had run, they found their piece had been killed. They called New York. *Why had the story not been used?* they wondered. *Was it too strong? Was there something wrong with it?* They told their boss in New York that they believed in the story's importance because it showed the real victims in the war, and added, "We don't want to be here if you are not going to put our stuff on the air."

Eric Sorensen, then-executive producer of the *Evening News,* took a long breath and replied: "The piece was fine, it really was, a pretty good piece—solid, moving. But you know, I just find that whole war over there very depressing."

CBS News turned away from foreign news so blindly that I could not even sell them on an interview with a then-little known Islamic activist named Osama bin Laden. In December 1996, producer Randall Joyce and I began contacts with a Saudi exile figure in London to arrange an interview with bin Laden in Afghanistan. The answer came back that bin Laden was ready to talk with CBS News for his first American interview. A *60 Minutes* team of correspondent Bob Simon and producer Mike Rosenbaum made similar approaches at the same time. In February, Joyce met another Saudi exile, who offered us the interview and told us to decide quickly which team should do it. That Saudi was later arrested and charged with being bin Laden's representative in

London and an accomplice in the American Embassy bombings in Africa.

In light of all that has happened since, I can still hardly believe that the interview never took place. The *60 Minutes* team
wasn't keen to move immediately, and the CBS News foreign
editor showed even less interest in my going. We argued that
this man would figure importantly in America's future. Joyce
and I saw that bin Laden was the leader of a terrorist network
bent on attacking American interests. Our bosses saw him as
an obscure Arab of no interest to our viewers. More concerned with saving dollars than pursuing the story, they killed
the project.

How, you might ask, could a news organization even judge
the importance of a figure like bin Laden, if not through the
advice of professionals like us whom they paid for precisely
this purpose? We understood that this man was at war with
America. But our bosses didn't wish to tell Americans that—
well, war didn't figure on their bottom-line agenda. I wish I
could say that they carefully weighed the implications before
making a judgment, that they came to a decision with America's future in mind. But I cannot exonerate them in any way.
They had their jobs in mind above all. As President Clinton
did, they too hoped the world would go away if they ignored it
long enough.

Still, bin Laden remained eager to raise his profile. So if
CBS wouldn't send us to Afghanistan to interview him, he
offered us a cheaper alternative. Our original Saudi contact
introduced us to a Syrian intermediary, who would do the interview for us at a fee of $25,000. Even that proved too ex-
pensive for CBS News, which turned down the offer. In the
end, ABC News and CNN both eventually landed bin Laden
interviews. CBS lost out, and I was crushed. I made one more

stab at doing the bin Laden story, this time from Saudi Arabia in April 1997. Joyce and I became the first television team to get into Prince Sultan Air Base and film the U.S. Air Force living there under enormous security—in a time of apparent peace and stability. By then, bin Laden had told the world several times that he considered the American military presence in Saudi Arabia to be an occupation of Islamic holy terrain, that he intended to make America suffer until it withdrew. Americans, of course, had little idea of the threat. We were at war with bin Laden—or at the very least he was at war with us—but the public knew nothing of it. On that same trip, Joyce used a hidden camera to interview a radical Islamist who drove him around the Saudi capital and happily confessed his readiness to blow up Americans living there. (Joyce refused his request to leave behind the hidden camera so this man could use it to film American installations and expatriate living compounds.)

It took weeks to set up that interview with the budding terrorist, and I am happy to say that CBS ran it as part of our series of reports from Saudi Arabia. We were told that it was a great story. However, despite his fulminations and successful terror attacks, bin Laden still couldn't get much attention from our navel-gazing executives. In one final effort to get bin Laden into our reports, I interviewed a London-based Arab journalist who had himself recently interviewed the Saudi terrorist in Afghanistan. He told us of bin Laden's hatred for America, of his violent intentions and dedicated followers. We put the results into one of our Saudi reports, but it ended up on the cutting-room floor; the *Evening News* told us to take out any mention of bin Laden. Why? Because there were "too many foreign names" in the story. CNN and ABC remain, to this day, very proud of their bin Laden interviews—as they should be. But *two interviews?* In all the years bin Laden spent advertising his antagonism toward America to all who would listen? In retrospect, the record hardly seems strong enough to merit much pride.

We foreign correspondents really couldn't fathom the situation back home. While we were witnessing firsthand a world of strife and danger, our bosses appeared to be living in a strange parallel universe. Their contradictory responses made no sense. They covered only major disasters abroad, yet turned down reports for being too depressing. We could see rising threats and coherent patterns pointing to catastrophe, and we saw the human consequences; all of it was simply waved away for incomprehensible reasons. Bad news was still real news sometimes, but more and more often it wasn't. The minute-by-minute pursuit of ratings by homebound executives induced in them a kind of hypnotized insularity that mystified us: We thought they lived in a fantasy world, and they thought the same of us.

To be fair, we could understand some of their reservations. The world abounded in awful incidents, political dramas, corruption and poverty, and much of it seemed to have no connection to the United States. Why even try to report it all? And why expect Americans to stay tuned? But often—too often—we *could* see the connections, and they just wouldn't. We had the expertise and experience to decipher developing dangers. That was our job. And that's where their insularity grew genuinely egregious. Well-informed executives should differentiate between more pointless bad news, and news that matters. If they can't, they should believe their correspondents. From that day to this, we are treated like supplicants at the gates, begging for funds, arguing our case in vain before indifferent superiors who, in turn, must answer to their corporate bosses with bottom-line arguments.

Take, for example, the case of the Kurds of northern Iraq. On the night that I did my first report, from London, on Saddam Hussein's 1988 poison gas attacks on the northern Iraq town of Halabja, the *Evening News* producer in charge of foreign news told me to take out the fact that the thousands of victims were all Kurds. *But that's what it's all about,* I shouted into the phone. The Kurds were being gassed because they were an ethnic minority being punished by Saddam for aiding his enemies, the Iranians. "Too confusing," was the *Evening News* verdict. "No one knows who the Kurds are." That sort of thinking would have reduced the Iraqi Kurds to permanent status as non-persons on CBS News, had they not figured so prominently in subsequent events in Iraq.

And there's the rub. It was surely obvious to any foreign news professional that the Kurds would feature more and more significantly in the region's affairs. During the first Gulf War, President George H. W. Bush had encouraged them to rise up against Saddam, then abandoned them to their fate. Turkey accepted some 200,000 of them as refugees, only to see its own Kurdish insurrection multiplied in the following years. Iran continued to use them as a proxy against Saddam. Finally, in the current war, Kurdish soldiers have fought alongside U.S. troops to suppress Sunni and Shi'ite uprisings. Kurdish minorities inhabit Iran, Syria, and Armenia, as well as Iraq and Turkey. To be ignorant of who they are, or of their potential strategic significance, is to do a serious, and willful, disservice to the Americans a news executive is supposed to serve.

Granted, complicated stories—especially ones that take place within foreign cultures—have to be explained and given context before the public can be counted on to understand and take interest in them. Too few executives have been ready to take on the challenge of making Americans understand context and relevance—a grievous omission. This is particularly true in a country such as ours, where the education system seems unable to teach history and geography effectively. Foreign news, by its very nature, requires the kind of cumulative context that only comes with long-term attention—in other words, more than just spot reporting. Why? Because world events have complex historical causes.

But long-term attention requires effort. And American news bosses simply don't have faith in the American public's attention span.

The ABC News program *Nightline,* which still does penetrating, intelligent journalism in a commercial television environment littered with trashy magazine shows, is proof that Americans will listen to well-prepared, well-explained, foreign news. Time and again, *Nightline*'s success disproves the lazy axiom of our business that stories from abroad—especially from Africa—spell death to ratings. Ted Koppel, the program's anchor, introduced one weeklong series called "The Heart of Darkness" from Goma, Congo, on September 7, 2001:

> At the heart of the continent, genocide in a tiny country; a genocide that horrified the world, brought chaos to a country almost 100 times its size. And you probably haven't heard a word. . . . It has claimed more lives than all the other current wars around the world combined. But outside of Africa, no one seems to have noticed. Three years, two and a half million dead. We thought someone should tell you.

Koppel was talking about Rwanda and the Congo, and the public listened. Tom Bettag, the show's executive producer, found to his own surprise that the show got a "terrific response": the ratings went way up. Bettag points out that no reliable data exist to prove that foreign news bores the viewing public—despite all the advice from consultants, and the self-serving protests from broadcast executives that paying for foreign news coverage is a costly extravagance that the public doesn't want anyway. Quoting his late mentor Fred Friendly, who resigned from the CBS News presidency on a matter of principle, Bettag reminds us: "When they say it isn't about the money, it's about the money."[4]

Depth of knowledge serves us in many ways: it helps to prevent our leaders from allying with special interests abroad without our knowledge, as the Clinton administration did with the Taliban in years prior to 9/11, and to prevent our newsmen from brainwashing us in favor of one side or another in foreign conflicts. Nobody mentions this last problem too loudly in the news business, but we need only recall how the American media (myself included) demonized the Serbs during the civil wars in former Yugoslavia. We left out the context that the ethnic Albanians, who were the victims in the 1990s, had themselves routinely slaughtered Serbs in World War II. And now that America has come to the Albanians' rescue, the Albanians are busy trying to ethnically cleanse Kosovo of all Serbs. If we are to prevent rather than merely react to violence—a common theme of George W. Bush's interventionist policies—then we need context early, especially as most of the time the problems will wash back onto our shores. We simply don't get enough informed foreign news to save our lives.

A direct line led from Somalia to 9/11 a decade later. What we now know is that al Qaeda battle-tested American resolve in Somalia: when we pulled out in the face of downed Black Hawks and airmen's bodies dragged through the streets, bin Laden deduced that he could strike with impunity over and over again. Which he did repeatedly, saying so in public declarations. The process unfolded visibly across the globe. With better background reporting, we could have understood, tracked, and anticipated—perhaps even saved American lives. At the very least, the news media could have made the Clinton administration pay more attention. (American diplomats in Africa warned for three years running that our embassies there were vulnerable. The administration did nothing.) Ultimately, the news media failed to collate a decade of hostile incidents into a pattern to tell us that, ready or not, we were already in a war.

They also failed to give us a coherent overview of developments, a strategic picture of events, as we'd had in the Cold War. Result: we continued to lose strategic ground against Islamic fundamentalism—the equivalent of letting the enemy occupy forward heights and pivotal positions in battle. They had a strategic awareness; we didn't. Hence, fundamentalists worked to gain footholds in conflicts such as Chechnya and Bosnia, which had started as secular civil wars with nationalist aims. Islamists provided indigenous Muslim warriors with money, arms and volunteers from outside—and a worldview to boot.

Consider the missed opportunity in all those post-Socialist, nominally Muslim entities from Asia to Europe, where local populations had almost entirely discarded their religious identities. They offered the potential for a vast secularized arc of Muslim states with a desire for westernized freedoms. The United States missed the chance to create a moderate Muslim bloc to counterbalance the appeal of fundamentalism. Instead, America let the jihadist movement grow and build credibility with every conflict, while our leaders in the news media let the region drop from their radar screens.

Through the 1990s, Islamists could point to a string of wars waged against their coreligionists from western China to Azerbaijan to Bosnia. They could show that Russia was allowed to reoccupy or cripple most of its newly independent Muslim republics, the so-called "Stans." For the first time in a century, Islamic ideologues could talk in terms of a crusade waged against the Muslim world by Russians, Serbians, Armenians in Azerbaijan, Chinese in western China, Indians in Kashmir and the like. It matters little that none of this was coordinated—as far as we know, but then we know so little. What matters is that Muslim fanatics could make the argument—and include America in their conspiracy theory. America was the world hegemon; nothing happened without our permission. Therefore America surely must have consented to the occupation of Muslim territories. Weren't U.S. forces occupying Saudi Arabia already? So the argument went. And it stuck.

Americans, of course, had no idea that any of this was brewing. The dots were never connected for them publicly; thus, in turn, there was no groundswell for public diplomacy against the trend, no concerted suggestion that we were allowing a new strategic threat to gain cohesion, size, and ideology.

To be sure, there were a few correspondents who sent up alarms: John Burns at the *New York Times* and Peter Bergen at CNN both did important reporting during these years. Yet their distress signals were obscured by endless pap about

Monica Lewinsky and O.J. Simpson and Princess Diana—a huge and indulgent mistake. America fiddled while the Muslim world smoldered, and eventually caught fire.

Central Asia was and still is a black hole for American news. Few reporters are sent there. In the mid-1990s, when the formerly Soviet central Asian republics were struggling to keep both Moscow and fundamentalism at bay, my late CBS News colleague Bill McClure was approached by a freelance journalist who was well versed in the region. Over the course of several decades, Bill had done scores of stories for *60 Minutes*; now, in his seventies, he pitched only the stories he found genuinely important. Together, Bill and his freelance colleague decided that this was a crucial story about a region that would play a determining role in the world's future.

Hemmed in by their borders with China, Afghanistan, Pakistan, and Russia, these now independent republics—Turkmenistan, Uzbekistan, Kazakhstan, Tajikistan—held large amounts of oil and gas. The Russians wanted to reassert control over their old possessions by denying them access to world markets for their raw materials, except through Russia. And how did the United States attempt to block that Russian strategy? By quietly cozying up to the Taliban, so that pipelines could be built from Central Asia through Afghanistan, free of Russian influence.

As the *Daily Telegraph* correspondent Ahmad Rashid detailed in his book *Jihad in Central Asia,* the Russians responded by fomenting their own Islamic fundamentalists against their previous colonies. That allowed Moscow to restation troops to "protect" the republics against what they called "destabilization." In short, they created an excuse for reoccupying these republics, which had been independent since the collapse of the Soviet Union. Russia and the

United States played a lethal backstairs game in that area during the 1990s—Russia forcefully, the United States rather drowsily—but the affair backfired for both countries. And most Americans remained ignorant of the entire episode. Together with his colleague, Bill McClure arranged for a meeting with *60 Minutes* correspondent Steve Kroft and pitched the idea.

Kroft's response? "Where exactly is Central Asia?"

Not so long ago, then, we were in a war but didn't know it. But we certainly do now. And we know, or should know, that Job One is the security and safety of our citizens. That doesn't necessarily mean colluding with the party that happens to dominate the government at any given moment; indeed, it might mean the precise opposite, if the government performs incompetently. What it does mean, emphatically, is that entertainment, celebrity gossip, mere scandal, and easy ratings coups must take a back seat on news broadcasts or on the front pages. It probably also means explicitly alerting the public to the new priorities, and explaining the reasons why our news must look and sound different from here on.

What exactly are the responsibilities of the news media in a time of war? Predictably, as with so much else, the news industry has missed this all-important topic, perhaps the most critical issue for public debate for our profession. What exactly should we do differently from before? Here's a list, with the clear understanding that it's hardly exhaustive or definitive—and, in my view, represents only things that we should have been doing all along.

1. Act as the public's early warning system, to danger from within our borders and without.
2. Monitor the government's performance in the service of our safety.
3. Make sure that the public knows what the government does abroad in our name.
4. Do not reveal information endangering the public or its defenders.
5. At the same time, do not be intimidated by censorship disguised as patriotism.
6. Do not shy away from educating the public in the historical and geographical contexts behind the news.
7. Train and select professionals competent in these tasks.
8. Make sure government does not abuse its powers at home.
9. Never allow the parent corporation's interests to prevail over the public's.
10. Help the country focus on the task at hand without trivial distractions.

Most of these may appear self-evident—and yet the news media fail to fulfill these assignments much of the time. To fulfill them consistently is not an easy task by any means, especially since some seem to contradict others. How, for example, can journalists act as watchdogs in a time of war without revealing strategic secrets? Take the case of nuclear power installations: an investigative report revealing flaws in their security might be of real public interest—but it might also help an enemy looking for targets. By the same token, how do you unveil abuses by our side without harming the morale of our troops? Abu Ghraib is a case in point: The media's total inattention during the early days of the scandal was replaced by sensationalistic saturation coverage once the story broke. Surely we can find a more balanced approach?

Wartime puts special pressures on the media as they monitor the government's performance. Journalists who pursue their rightful role to probe, investigate, and criticize the government are too easily, and often unfairly, accused of a lack of patriotism, as Peter Jennings knows firsthand. In the months preceding the Iraq war, Jennings says, he felt the heat from conservatives who did not like his coverage of Iraq: "*World News Tonight* was regarded as the most critical [of the networks], and it made people in the shop—some people in the shop—a little bit nervous, because the vocalness of the conservatives in the country is very considerable, and it spooks some people a little bit. When the war began to turn out less like the conventional wisdom thought it was going to turn out, and our pre-war analysis looked a little more intelligent, there was a little less criticism."

Jennings realizes that this kind of reaction is part of the job. "There is no doubt if you go on the Internet, and look up Rather or Jennings or Brokaw or Fenton or whatever, you will find a good number of people who think we are the scum of the earth. I am always interested in it; I don't seek it out to punish myself, but I think it's always important to be aware of it. I was going to the Democratic Convention in Boston, and a man walked past me on the aisle. I smiled and said good morning, and he passed again. As we were getting out of the plane he stopped in the middle of the aisle and said to me, 'You should leave the country. You are a disgrace.' Well, it shocked me and shocked a lot of people who were sitting around me. But in some respects it was a good thing to have that happen to me." Another time, Jennings was interviewing people in Dallas, Texas; when he asked them to tell him what they felt was right and wrong with the country, one man told him *"You're* wrong with the country." This time, Jennings was able to make use of the barb. "Not being thoroughly stupid, I put it on the air—thereby eliciting tons and tons of mail from people in Texas on the other side."

Of course, the media aren't always the good guys. As CBS News's Don Hewitt admits, "We do act too big for our breeches, and do have an exaggerated sense of our own importance." Naturally, mistakes by the news media appear much more obvious after the fact. It's easy to be a Monday morning quarterback. But the behavior of the news media in the 1990s amounts to more than a few stray mistakes; it represents a pattern of fundamental misjudgment that played out over a long period of time. The industry might have a better alibi if it had spent those years increasing the resources available to its hard news organizations, or if it displayed any real concern over threats to the homeland—in short, if its sense of public duty had visibly come before corporate calculations. As the evidence shows, the reverse is true.

On some nights prior to 9/11, the network news shows featured no foreign news at all. The was a major shift from the heyday of network news in the 1970s, when the networks dominated the airwaves—and almost half the content of most network evening news broadcasts was devoted to foreign news. The same phenomenon occurred in the newspaper business: foreign news fell from 10 percent of the average daily's news content in 1971 to roughly 2 percent [by 9/11]. The major news magazines cut back their foreign news from 22 percent in 1985 to 13 percent in 1995.[5] And yet the popularity of news broadcasts fell consistently throughout those years. The more they dumbed down in the race for ratings, the more viewers they lost.

And no wonder: When skimpier news resources chase an ever more unstable world, the outcome is a kind of herd reporting where all reporters and news channels chase after the same Big Story, or Big Scandal, and neglect the rest. Such a strategy may help a network to cut costs, but in the end it can only alienate the public, which will not be fooled for ever. Indeed, some studies show that news executives who downplayed foreign news were seriously out of touch with their audience. In a poll conducted shortly before 9/11 by the Pew Research Center and the Council on Foreign Relations, the public ranked protecting the United States from terrorist attacks as the top foreign policy priority. A 1999 study by the Gallup Organization found that most Americans believed the twenty-first century would be even bloodier than the twentieth.[6] But the gatekeepers were looking at other studies: Their corporate accountants kept pointing out that foreign stories cost at least twice as much as domestic stories, and no one managed to mount a strong enough counterargument to turn the tide.

It wouldn't have taken any special research or investigation for the news executives to get the message about terrorism, either. There was already a highly credible government commission at work trying to alert America to the dangers. In January 2001, the U.S. Commission on National Security, chaired by former Senators Gary Hart and Warren Rudman, warned that international terrorism was a direct threat to the United States, and that "Americans will likely die on American soil, possibly in large numbers." Few news organizations paid attention to the commission.

We are now in the midst of a war that was triggered by exactly that event—a large number of Americans killed in just the way the Hart-Rudman Commission predicted. Yet the industry's structural fundamentals have not changed. Indeed, the networks have almost gone out of the foreign news gathering business. The foreign bureaus they had closed before 9/11 have not been re-opened; the networks remain complacently content to "package" a lot of canned news in London, with all the compromises that process entails. No one batted an eye when CBS News followed ABC's example in 2004 and decided it no longer needed a resident correspondent in Russia—a country with a rusting nuclear arsenal, an acute terrorism problem, and an increasingly authoritarian leader. *U.S. News and World Report* has closed all its foreign bureaus—making one wonder how its editors can justify calling their magazine a "world report" at all. The news purveyors still serve their pockets before the public.

Which is why, in the list of wartime principles to be followed by news media, I left to last—item 10—the most controversial and perhaps the most important item, one that the average citizen might take for granted. Few present-day journalists would even think of it, and most would cringe at anything that smells of wartime cheerleading. Yet real danger threatens our country directly. Tom Ridge, the inept Homeland Security chief who quit after the Bush administration's first term, could certainly have used our help, partly because he so signally failed to inspire or rouse the nation to vigilance. As in any war, morale and the public psyche matter crucially—and in that arena the media play a decisive role. The merest news report of a threat has more effect than any change in the government-mandated color-coded alert levels.

Many journalists would urge extreme caution against taking up such an overtly patriotic role. But that misses the point: Defending the homeland is not the same thing as supporting the war in Iraq or the incumbent administration. Indeed, often it requires criticizing, prodding, probing for deficiencies in government. It certainly involves helping the country stay focused in stretches of time when threats no longer seem imminent. And to some extent the news media is still turning out reporting of that kind: investigations into the safety of ports and coasts, probing of airline security systems, and the like. But public consciousness of homeland security today hardly compares to the levels it reached during World War II.

And every day four thousand illegal aliens cross our southern border.

After 9/11, our elected officials urged Americans to go back to business as usual. President Bush told Americans to "get on the airlines, get about the business of America," announcing improved security measures on commercial flights. Astonishingly, they even urged us "to go shopping": New York's suddenly omnipresent mayor, Rudolph Giuliani, said that his shocked city needed "the best shoppers in the world" to return to restaurants, Broadway shows, and stores. Such concerns were understandable: Bush, Giuliani, and the like naturally didn't want the economy to seize up or the country to be paralyzed with fear in the wake of those unprecedented attacks. But the status-quo response from these and other government officials was a clear signal that they had no intention of mobilizing the entire nation to a war footing, post-Pearl Harbor style. Perhaps they doubted the public's potential response to a call for a unified national effort, but to Americans disoriented by such a universal shock, it was strange and disturbing to have their leaders urge them to work it off with a trip to the mall. It trivialized the threat, and sent the subliminal message that our government really didn't want us participating in their business too closely. It was hardly surprising that, within months, many began to doubt our leaders' motives.

For those of us in the hard news business, of course, going back to business as usual should have been the last thing on our minds. With a government that has failed to mobilize or unify the country, it falls to the media to take up the slack. If anything, the Bush administration's record shows a willful, combative divisiveness; its us-versus-them attitude has alienated not only our former allies but many average Americans—this at a time when the world and the country need precisely the opposite from the president of the United States. As Andrew Sullivan, the former editor of *The New Republic* and right-of-center commentator, recently wrote: "I believe in this war, which is why I believe it is important to get as many Democrats to support it. But the Republicans have all but declared that this is a Republican war—and can only be conducted by a Republican President. I fear the animosity and division that are already part of the cultural fabric could get worse in the coming years— to the glee of our enemies. In wartime, unity matters. When a campaign deliberately tries to maximize polarization to its advantage, it undermines the war. Winning this war is more important than building a new Republican majority."

I am not sure that this is a war that can be "won" in the traditional sense—with a V-Day style celebration or symbolic tearing down of a Berlin wall; indeed, it's not even clear that it is a war in the classic sense of the word. But it is already a dangerous campaign and will undoubtedly become a long one. And it is not one we can learn to fight willy-nilly, like the British campaign against the IRA in Northern Ireland, or the Spanish campaign against the Basque separatists, until it someday burns itself out. If we are to fight it successfully, the news media have a role to perform: to help focus and unify Americans for the long haul, without pandering to authorities determined to run their own private war, both here and abroad.

We live in strange times. For a decade, our leaders in Washington comforted us with the pretense that we were not at war. Now they are trying to wage war without waking us up. The media fell for it once. We must not do so again.

CHAPTER THREE

HOW WE GOT HERE

In 1940, the famous wit and early New Yorker writer A. J. Liebling returned to a still slumbering America from a long stay in Europe, which was already enduring the death and despair of World War II. The carefree mood in this country astonished him. He felt as if he had flown in from another planet. With Hitler about to overrun the continent, England cornered and losing, Liebling recognized that the United States would surely be the next target. Yet nobody seemed inclined to listen to stories of the trouble overseas, or worry much that it would land in their own backyard.[1]

"Getting off the plane and meeting people who had stayed in America was a strange experience," Liebling wrote, "because they hardly seemed to know that anything was wrong." Friends told him to relax and take a sleeping pill or two, get a few good nights of sleep, maybe go to the horse races, have some fun, and he'd get over all those awful things he'd seen abroad. "It was like a dream," wrote Liebling, "in which you yell at people and they don't hear you." The only people he met who seemed the least concerned about the war were the officers he met at the War Department when he went to Washington to do a profile of General George Marshall.

After he had been back for a while, Liebling wrote, he "began to get stupid too"—growing a little bored by the hysteria of new arrivals from Europe. Dick Boyer, who had been an American newspaper correspondent in Berlin, told him about the bombings he had lived through. Boyer had only been back two days and "still looked at people in astonishment, because they did not seem worried enough."

To some degree, Americans have always lived as though dissociated from the world beyond. Virtually every other country on the globe knows the horrors of being invaded and marauded by outsiders. The last time such a thing happened to us was 1814. The threat or memory of invasion has never much shaped our thoughts, informed our songs or myths. Others have had to learn the hard lessons of geography and history firsthand. We have never needed to. America the safe haven and America the self-absorbed, even the self-righteous America that assumes the right to impose enlightenment on foreign nations: All of these are part of the same package. Foreign correspondents coming home almost always feel that strange sensation Liebling experienced, marveling at how much better attuned to world currents are the people we meet around the world.

As recent events have demonstrated, we can no longer afford such ignorance. But we still haven't fully awakened to our new condition.

As a nation, the zenith of our awareness ran from World War II through the Cold War. Why? Because our newly powerful media, flexing their muscles for the first time, had invested massively in gaining that knowledge. That period marked the high point of foreign news, when American newspapers and networks had bureaus and correspondents around the world. In those years, CBS News put more resources into covering Paris than Chicago. From the collapse of communism until the attacks of 9/11, the networks showed little or no interest in the rest of the world—and even 9/11, as we shall see, caused only a temporary halt in the decline of foreign newsgathering. We are today still a long way from the heyday of foreign news, even with the addition of the CNN, Fox News, and MSNBC 24-hour news channels. The withdrawal from foreign coverage has been felt across the board in the American news media, but most noticeably in television.

There are a number of reasons for this reduction, reasons that at first might seem, from the corporate shareholders' point of view, perfectly sound. They have been described in the memoirs of my colleagues over the years, and endless round-table discussions have allowed correspondents and anchors to lament them at length—to no effect whatsoever. It's what I call the "Nothing Can Be Done Syndrome." Below I list some of the most popular talking points that arise during such discussions—points you've probably heard somewhere yourself. Each of these points reflects a real problem. Those problems should be understood, and deplored. But we must no longer accept them as an adequate excuse. And be warned: I wouldn't use heavy machinery while reading them, for these timeworn excuses can induce a sense of drowsy helplessness. They've certainly affected the nation's alertness. Every one of these excuses has long seemed like an immutable law of nature—but only because the industry thought them immutable. That strongly suggests that we cannot look to the industry to change itself from within. The public must get involved and make demands. Get angry, be skeptical, and don't let these reasons convince you that nothing can be done. Here they are:

1. The status of news as a profit earner
2. The deregulation of broadcasting
3. The decline of the industry's codes of standards
4. The obsession with ratings
5. The expense of maintaining foreign bureaus
6. The growth of packaging, rather than gathering, news
7. The corporate ownership of the news media

To take them one by one:

THE STATUS OF NEWS AS A PROFIT EARNER

When I first went to work for CBS News in the Rome Bureau in 1970, nobody talked about news making a profit. The news helped fulfill the requirements of the Federal Communications Commission that, in return for free use of the airwaves, television stations should air programs providing a public service. The networks didn't even bother trying to save money. We hired Lear jets and zoomed around the world as if covering the news was the only thing that counted.

I was astonished at how much we correspondents spent. At one point, I even sent a message to Bob Little, a hard-drinking, hard-driving, old-school CBS News foreign editor, suggesting ways to save a few dollars. The answer snapped back on the telex: "Fenton you are in the news covering business, not the cost cutting business." Nothing mattered more than the news itself, except perhaps beating the competition, and throughout the 1970s and much of the 1980s, CBS News was unbeatable.

The networks expected their news divisions to bring prestige rather than profits to the owners, running them as loss leaders, an important part of the branding of their corporations. The late William S. Paley, founder and chairman of CBS, was famously quoted as telling his correspondents, "You worry about the news. I've got Jack Benny to bring in the profits."

It was that climate that gave birth in 1968 to one of the most profitable and widely watched programs on American television: *60 Minutes*. Don Hewitt, the creator and executive producer, tells the story.

"I was doing documentaries. And I realized that people watch documentaries, both the good ones and the bad ones, because they are *called* documentaries. Some were great, some were terrible, but they had the same percentage of the audience—in other words, the documentary crowd, about seven percent of the audience. I knew there had to be a better way to reach people with significant events.

"One day I had lunch with Norman Isaacs, when he was running the *Louisville Courier-Journal,* and he said, 'You know how many newspaper readers read editorials?' I said no. He said, 'Seven per cent.' I thought, oh my God, they're the people who watch documentaries." But another statistic Isaacs shared with Hewitt made a far bigger impression: 90 percent of readers reported that they read columnists.

That clicked with Hewitt. "I said, 'Here's the problem: Nobody is interested in the voice of the corporation.'" At the time, each of the networks had a documentary series branded with the network imprimatur: *CBS Reports, NBC White Paper, ABC Close Up*. As Hewitt realized, "They're [like] the editorials. They don't read them. That's what the *company* is telling them." What was missing was a more independent, and thus credible, voice. "If you make it personal journalism—and I don't mean advocacy journalism—and package reality as well as Hollywood packages fiction," Hewitt thought, "I bet we can raise the seven percent to ten or eleven percent. We not only raised it—in all the history of television, only three broadcasts were ever number one for the year five times: Bill Cosby, Archie Bunker, and *60 Minutes*. We spent twenty-two years in the top ten. Nobody will ever come anywhere close to that."

Besides shaking off the old corporate mantle, *60 Minutes* also achieved an attractive new blend of news and entertainment. "I know that there are those who think that entertainment is a bad word," Hewitt says. But mixing in a little show business helped draw viewers to *60 Minutes* every Sunday night. Hewitt recalls: "I directed *See It Now,* Murrow's class operation. It didn't have many viewers and it went off the air. But Murrow's *Person to Person,* when he visited celebrities at home, was a smash hit. And one day in the *New York Herald Tribune* the television critic coined a phrase: He called it 'high Murrow and low Murrow.' And I thought, my God, that's the answer. You put high Murrow and low Murrow in the same broadcast, you've got a winner. You can look in Marilyn Monroe's closet. You can also look in Robert Oppenheimer's laboratory. You gotta do both."

It was a practice, Hewitt realized, that other segments of the media had been employing for years. "The guys who knew that first were at *Life* magazine," he says. "*Life* was my Bible. *Life* was on every coffee table in America because of [its] covers. I said, *I* need covers—and *CBS Reports* is not a cover. *NBC White Paper* is not a cover. Mike Wallace's face is a cover. Harry Reasoner's face is a cover. And it took off."

The enormous success—and profitability—of *60 Minutes* didn't go unnoticed by the networks. Everything began to change when the networks discovered in the late 1970s that they could make serious money from news.[2] News became the "news business." At CBS, the news division went from being considered the jewel in the crown to being what accountants call a *profit center.* Over the years, all three networks gradually ditched chunks of their hard-news commitments like so many bags of ballast to lighten and liberate the balance sheet. And as the Soviet threat faded, they virtually ditched foreign news, leaving only enough behind to give the illusion that they were still in the foreign news-gathering business. With sports contracts almost prohibitively expensive, and hit entertainment increasingly costly to develop, lightweight news is relatively cheap to put on the air and can make a substantial contribution to the bottom line—especially if the networks, and the corporations that own them, can pare costs and keep the federal regulators off their backs. They have been notably successful at doing both.

THE DEREGULATION OF BROADCASTING

In the 1980s, under intense lobbying by the networks, the Federal Communications Commission, which is supposed to represent the public's interest, began to deregulate broadcasting. The FCC increased the number of stations the networks can own, and dropped the requirement for public service broadcasting. Network news shows were now free to cut corners and chase ratings to their heart's content. As Lawrence Grossman, the former head of PBS and NBC News, observes, the FCC has always been a paper tiger, and rarely pulled a station's license:

"The people who run these corporations, they don't have to worry about losing their [broadcasting] license. They are judged on one thing and one thing only: How did they do this quarter versus last quarter? It's ratings, because [that's what] brings in the advertising and the money." Grossman notes ruefully that the networks' one-time commitment to public responsibility has become no more than "a lot of rhetoric." "Every time the broadcasters are threatened with limits on the number of stations they can own, or being required to give free time to candidates, they wrap themselves around the first amendment and say that's violating our right to decide for ourselves—the government is interfering in what news should be."

THE DECLINE OF THE INDUSTRY'S CODES OF STANDARDS

The old edition of the *CBS News Standards,* issued in 1976, contained a preface by the late Richard Salant, president of the news division. Salant was not a newsman but a lawyer, and he was a stickler who defined the dictates of news ethics with the precision of a contract. Sometimes we correspondents thought he went too far: If you missed a camera shot when a subject entered the room, you could not ask the person to do it again. More important, Salant refused to waver on essential principles and on our duty to the public. In the standards guide he wrote, he drew a line of integrity that none of us could cross:

> We in broadcast journalism cannot, should not, and will not base our judgments on what we think the viewers and listeners are "most interested" in, or hinge our news judgment and our news treatment on our guesses or someone else's surveys as to what news the people want to hear and see, and in what form. The judgments must be professional news judgments—nothing more, nothing less.[3]

That warning has disappeared from the latest version of the *CBS News Standards*—a document that talks about "accuracy" and "fairness," but seems to overlook that we owe more than that to the public. In today's world, it may sound unrealistically elitist, even arrogant, to insist that professional journalists are best qualified to decide what news the public needs. You could make that argument to sell a story in the old days, and sometimes win. Nowadays, instead of using their best news judgment, television executives hire consultants who go from station to station peddling their version of what they think the public wants.

Sanford Socolow, who was the executive producer of the *CBS Evening News* in the days of Walter Cronkite, describes how it all started under a "news consultant" named Frank Magid. Magid, he says, "gave advice to local news stations—on the acceptability of on-air persons, on what kinds of stories to air. He used to tell them not to bother covering city hall because it was boring." Out of this philosophy, Socolow observes, came a new maxim: "If it bleeds, it leads."

With this new philosophy came a flood of soft news. Longtime *Evening News* anchor Dan Rather says that CBS doesn't hire consultants. But he concedes that their influence is nevertheless felt on the network level.

"It started permeating in the eighties," Rather says. "If it was around before that, I wasn't aware of it. Leading stations, including some of the largest stations, brought in consultants to help their ratings out. And word spread quickly when somebody's ratings moved. If you went from third to first in a month, a lot of people—including television writers—noticed." Rather hints at the negative implications of consultant influence on the news business. "I hate to use the word 'infect,'" he says. "But you don't have to have consultants in your newsroom or on your broadcast for them to have influence."

The race for ratings is well understood, Rather notes. But as he points out, the old pure-market-share benchmark has now been replaced by the more challenging "demographic imperative." "We're at the point now where even if you do well in the ratings—that is, how many homes tune in at a given time—it doesn't end the pressure. Because what now they sell on are the demographics. The preferred demographic is eighteen-to-forty-nine, and within that the platinum demographic is males eighteen-to-twenty-four, because it's hard to get them to try television."

On average, the network evening news shows air one story per night that originates beyond our shores. Some nights they offer no foreign news at all. We have all heard a lot of talk in recent years about the "liberal elites" who determine the content and bias of news. Indeed, it has become a mindless cliché, one that contains just enough truth to confuse the real issue. The fact is, the news will always be filtered by groups of journalists at the top—an elite by definition, whether they lean to the left or the right. You can't get rid of elites: they are part of nature. But elites should have a code of integrity and a transparency that keeps them honest and wedded to high standards.

The angle of their bias *should* be monitored and spotlighted from without. And far more important is this simple fact: the less real news they supply, the fewer choices the public will have, and the more effective their bias will be.

THE OBSESSION WITH RATINGS

Ratings are the new standards that have replaced the old code of public responsibility in the networks' mindset. If the media executives feel any responsibility now, it's to the bottom line. Higher ratings mean networks and news stations can charge higher rates for commercials. Instead of referring to a code of standards for quality broadcasting, news broadcasters hire consultants and commission audience research studies. I was shocked when I learned that the networks now have the power to measure the number of listeners minute by minute. Rather told me that CBS News uses these minute-by-minute ratings, "but I do not see them and I am not sure the executive producer sees them." You can imagine how they affect the choice of stories the news shows air. The instant an anchor utters the word Azerbaijan or Indonesia, he's fighting against a ticking meter of declining viewers. The overall result is a shrinking amount of foreign news, and an endless flow of "news you can use"—medical stories, consumer news—and the kind of frivolous and sensational fare that used to be limited to the tabloids.

The average evening broadcast now includes fewer than nineteen minutes of news—and the figure keeps dropping as the broadcasts squeeze in more promotions and commercials. Once you get past the first half of the show, the rest tends to consist of features aimed at delivering viewers to advertisers. How else can you explain why the *CBS Evening News* of August 11, 2004, with Scott Pelley sitting in for Dan Rather as anchor, turned down a story from the London bureau on the British government's groundbreaking decision to allow Newcastle University to clone human embryos for medical research? The decision put Britain in the vanguard of a technology with the potential to produce cures for such diseases as Parkinson's, diabetes, and Alzheimer's. Stem-cell research raises major ethical questions, which Americans certainly do care about: Californians voted for state-funded stem-cell research in the 2004 national election. Exactly how much Americans care even surprised the presidential candidates when it became one of the hot button issues in the 2004 presidential campaign.

The *CBS Evening News* apparently felt the cloning story wasn't worth reporting, but did find room for a lengthy story revisiting the invasion of Asian carp in American rivers and lakes—and even a self-indulgent, tongue-in-cheek interview with *60 Minutes* correspondent Mike Wallace. The segment described Wallace's run-in with a couple of New York Taxi & Limousine Commission inspectors who had warned his chauffeur about double-parking while Wallace was buying a take-out order of meatloaf. The public learned that Wallace also got a summons for arguing with the inspectors, but Americans were no doubt relieved to hear that the meatloaf tasted fine after he'd reheated it in the microwave. The Pelley-Wallace interview ran for one minute and fifty-two seconds— long, by *Evening News* standards. Without it, the stem-cell story might have made it, but who cares about such things? (Incidentally, ABC's *World News Tonight* kissed off the stem-cell story with a nineteen-second "tell"; *NBC Nightly News*, like CBS, ignored it altogether.)

News driven by popularity poll naturally affects content, but it also corrupts the presentation and style of hard news. Jazzing up hard news *sounds* like a good idea: In principle I'm all for attempts to make foreign reporting interesting and accessible, since in my view our own failure to keep the public interested partly explains why the accountants and programming gurus have been able to take over so thoroughly. Sadly, though, the same mentality that degrades all news also determines how to make hard news popular, and it's all based on a contempt for the audience's intelligence. Sound-bite snippets, emotional "moments," pandering to the star system—such methods assume that the dumbed-down audience will only respond to showbiz techniques. How about simply explaining why an item of foreign news matters, how it affects the audience's lives, why they should care? In other words, *CONTEXT, CONTEXT, CONTEXT!*

Instead, during the Afghan war for example, Fox News offered us Geraldo Rivera and an array of intrepid, inexperienced blondes to cover the combat zone firsthand. What's wrong with that? Don't get me started. You can imagine how veteran foreign correspondents, and veteran Afghanistan experts in the field, felt when that army of clueless *journos* started stampeding all over the war zone. American news organizations had so depleted the ranks of hard news reporters over the years that they suddenly had to send out whatever lifestyle, fashion, and gossip types they could muster on a moment's notice—plus, of course, a few Big Names who knew far more about grandstanding than they did about Afghanistan.

Let's take Geraldo and his style of parachute journalism as an example. One veteran *Newsweek* Beirut correspondent remembers a revealing story about Geraldo during the fierce 1980s Lebanese civil war. A long bout of shelling had caught a group of veteran correspondents in Yassir Arafat's bunker. (In those days, Arafat and the PLO were based in Beirut.) After several hours, the shelling stopped and the journalists came out to breathe. During the lull, says the former *Newsweek* man, "we saw someone screech up in a taxi with a television crew. It was Geraldo Rivera. He came charging out and looked around wildly until he found a young boy playing in the distance. He brought him around in front of the bunker and, kneeling down next to him, began telling of how terrified innocents such as these were in danger from this war. Fair enough, but the boy had been nowhere near the fighting—and neither had Geraldo."

In the same vein, during the post-9/11 Afghanistan war, wherever Geraldo popped up he incessantly invoked the danger and risk of his work. If not, the Fox News anchor would prompt him to do so. On one occasion at the famous Khyber Pass, which links Pakistan to Afghanistan, Geraldo did an on-camera piece about the dangers of being in that place. In fact, scores of journalists had passed through there unmolested in the previous weeks, because the Pakistani government had opened the pass and reinforced it with troops, and the Taliban had fled from the Afghan side.

As for the "Fox Lovelies," as some called them, Fox News was hardly the only offender. The networks discovered early that the presence of a fair and comely reporter among scowling tribesmen and falling bombs could add *frisson* to the broadcast. The *Wall Street Journal* ran a sly commentary by op-ed page features editor Tunku Varadarajan about which network offered us the most attractive "correspondette." He caught a lot of flak from feminist pundits, who missed the humor and the point. Varadarajan simply took the news organizations at face value: If they chose female charm as a criterion for assignment, he would judge them by it. Some of the best foreign correspondents I know are women, but the ones I admire the most were chosen for their smarts, not their looks.

Ultimately, there's nothing inherently wrong with the use of populist gimmickry to attract ratings—as long as the audience benefits in the process through better information, more in-depth reporting, and better access to the truth. But the television stars of the Afghan war, with their support staffs, were unlikely to uncover anything unexpected. Producers threw around so much money so irresponsibly into the local economy that selling dodgy tips and questionable video to the networks became a cottage industry for the natives. Independent journalists with small budgets complained they couldn't afford to pay off tribesmen, and that no local would volunteer information based on truth when they could get money for any serviceable lie. Ultimately the public understood very little of the war, beyond what we in the business call "bang-bang" (or, in Afghanistan, the distant "boom-boom" of bombs on hillsides). Not a clue to bin Laden's whereabouts. No indications of whether he's alive or dead. Even the host of *America's Most Wanted* came up empty-handed.

THE EXPENSE OF MAINTAINING FOREIGN BUREAUS

When hired consultants tell the networks that viewers dislike foreign news, they push against an open door. Network bean counters love to close down foreign bureaus—which are very expensive, and produce stories that rarely get aired—precisely because the networks have such a limited appetite for foreign news. It's a vicious circle.

You may have heard about the cutbacks in news-gathering resources, but I doubt if the general public knows how far they have gone. When I first went to work for CBS News, we had a Rome bureau staffed by three correspondents. Now we have only three foreign bureaus staffed by correspondents in the entire world. In its heyday in the late 1970s and early 1980s, CBS News ran fourteen major foreign bureaus, ten mini-foreign bureaus, and stringers in forty-four countries around the world. Now, CBS has a total of eight foreign correspondents—four of them in London (where most of the foreign news is packaged), one who lives in Rome when not on the road, two in Tel Aviv, and one in Tokyo. Baghdad was opened as a temporary bureau, as was Kabul, both staffed by visiting correspondents and likely to be closed as soon as American troops leave. CBS News no longer keeps correspondents in Germany, France,

Eastern Europe, Moscow, Cairo, Beirut, Nairobi, Johannes-
burg, Beijing, Hong Kong, or any of the other places that it
once staffed. Most surprising of all, there are no permanent
CBS News correspondents in the Arab world or the Muslim
world at large—not even in Pakistan, where experts think bin
Laden has been hiding most of the time. You might think that
would be a good place to keep an eye on. CBS News did all of
three stories from Pakistan in 2003.

The networks' normal practice now is to fly a news team
into a country and place a correspondent in front of a camera before he has time to get his feet wet. And they assume
the public won't know the difference. Well, *of course* the public doesn't notice—because it's used to being underserved. A
news organization that closes down a bureau loses its eyes
and ears on the ground. The best it can do is to react to
events in that country. As Walter Cronkite, the dean of American broadcast journalists, warns, there are profound dangers to this practice: "This whole idea of parachuting
correspondents and camera crews into a place where there is
a crisis, that's too late. When you parachute people in, the
fire is already burning." Cronkite notes that those fires are
often burning in "distant countries where we [the public]
don't know the location on the map and don't even know
how to pronounce the names"—and, as he warns, "those
bonfires can easily turn into mushroom shaped clouds today,
if we don't call attention to them [and alert] the free nations
[to] take action."

As for Geraldo-style easy-on easy-off journalism,
Cronkite doesn't put much stock in it. If you're one of those
"parachuting correspondents," he muses, "what [do you] do
on arrival at this capital which we have found out exists? You
go to the stringer that you have, a name that you haven't

heard from for five or ten years anyway—but that individual almost invariably in those countries works for a newspaper or the state broadcasting system. They are already committed to a point of view, and when you ask them for sources— who can I talk to?—they are going to send you to the person who is going to tell you the official story, or the story carried by their newspaper." Then, after being "misled for the first several days . . . the correspondent realizes what is happening and gets to some sources other than the stringer's, and that takes a few days"—but by that time, chances are, "there are no headlines, so they are pulled out."

Cronkite hints at how inexperienced reporters often rely on preconceived storylines. But that kind of thing isn't limited to stringers: When the home office sends reporters abroad, they do so to report an already conceived story, not to go out and find one they may not know about. Hence they seldom uncover fresh stories. Nor are they likely to dig up much that's new from an office thousands of miles away. The networks closed their overseas bureaus because they could get away with it—especially given the massive improvements in instant communication technology, from satellite uplinks to the Internet. Anchors could interview heads of state across the globe without leaving their desks. The *illusion* of global coverage could continue. A few star faces, such as Christiane Amanpour, could still be seen zooming around the globe. After all, that's what dumbed-down American audiences responded to: celebrity journalists who humanized or glamorized the news simply by their presence—or so the consultants argued. Instead of an experienced correspondent who knows the local culture and news sources, networks now rely mostly on news agencies, primarily the Associated Press and Reuters, to provide video and news. It's a lot cheaper.

THE GROWTH OF PACKAGING, RATHER
THAN GATHERING, NEWS

It used to be the other way around: The American networks provided news coverage to the world. CBS had its own syndication service, with correspondents and stringers around the world. NBC fed stories to Visnews, and ABC fed to United Press International Television News (UPITN). Now the networks rely increasingly on packaging news gathered by someone else, and they do most of the packaging of foreign news from London. Were it not for the London signoff, you might think the correspondent is actually in Africa, or some other place the networks no longer cover. Flip through the channels, and you'll find that all the networks routinely use the same video—purchased from the agencies, which often lift it from the local television of a foreign country. Consider the contempt for the intelligence of American viewers that such a practice implies. The networks treat the London sign-off as adequate—because, after all, *it's foreign*. The folks back home don't see the difference in a story from Kuala Lumpur reported from London: It's all out there somewhere, isn't it? London correspondents (myself included) have been known to go to the trouble of doing standups in front of the big mosque in St. John's Wood—because it doesn't *look* like London.

But even when the correspondent does a standup in Baghdad, that may be his only video contribution to the story. The rest of the segment likely came from agency footage, and was cobbled together in London by the producer assigned to "catch" the Baghdad piece that night. When things got really bad in Iraq, most correspondents decided the better part of valor required them to remain in the hotel and do their standups in the garden or on the roof.[4] How much real reporting could they do under the circumstances? How much of the story in Iraq, or Afghanistan, were they—and the viewers—missing by not being there? The answer is: plenty.

Peter Jennings says that today Iraq is the hardest story he works on. "The lack of coverage in Iraq is distressing. The greatest influence I have had at the shop over the last few weeks and months, I think, is to encourage them—not force them—to say we have to do x, y, and z in order to get daily coverage on Iraq. Because the audience—especially the conservatives—say we are doing a bad job covering Iraq, and they are right. They are absolutely right. We are not doing a good job covering Iraq." Yet, for Jennings, the answer seems to be to depend more on accepting secondhand video: "We have to rely more on the Arab satellite channels. You know, don't dismiss them. Some of them know the story better than us, in many respects. We have to find every in-country reporter out there and get them on the air every day, even if it is only for a soundbite."

The networks' practice of packaging stories they didn't cover can also lead to omissions and errors. When a news organization uses video and information from an agency, the correspondent rarely knows who actually gathered it. Often it's a local journalist or cameraman who may be reluctant to ruffle the feathers of the officials in his country, and at worst may have an agenda. As Walter Cronkite points out, "The problem is that you—that is, the organization that is accepting the service or the report—have lost control. You are only circulating something that is already available, not checking those facts against your own expert reporters." To Cronkite, there's a thin line between that kind reporting and what he calls monopoly journalism: "If Reuters or AP is the only one to get the story, that's a single source, and we should be double checking it."

The network that broadcasts the story puts its own logo on it, but the surmounting logo scarcely guarantees the story's authenticity. We will never know how many errors creep into broadcasts that way, because the networks rarely have the time or facilities to verify the agency footage, and very rarely do they broadcast corrections.

There is another kind of packaging—the packaging of news shows. From the days of radio to the present, news broadcasts have always been just that: shows. News channels are in the business of creating product both for viewers and for advertisers. Every day, their product needs to be selected, edited, sequenced, and bundled into neat and tidy productions. The executive producer has to decide what downbeat story to place next to which commercial, followed by a more uplifting segment, and piece it all together into a coherent reassuring whole. There's nothing new in that. But that doesn't make it right. The world is not neat and tidy, and the packaging of shows skews the news. The news boss often selects stories on the basis of how well they "fit" the flow of the show, not on their real importance in the events of the day. More than once have I been told by a *CBS Evening News* producer that my contribution would lead the newscast that day (because the show needed a hard news piece for the top), only to see my story dropped altogether when some bigger story came along—not because it wasn't news anymore, but because it didn't "fit" anymore.

At first, it seemed as though the twenty-four-hour news channels—CNN, MSNBC, and Fox News—would offer a more flexible format capable of reflecting the world's vicissitudes more closely. But they too soon fell into formulaic programming, interrupted periodically by nonstop coverage of crises, both real and imagined. CNN rightly earned enormous kudos during the first Gulf War for its round-the-clock reporting. By the time of the second war, however, Fox News's jingoistic challenge had pushed CNN towards celebrity anchors and other gimmicks, which is where they are stuck today. Meanwhile, studio-edited production values continue to triumph over good journalism.

THE CORPORATE OWNERSHIP OF THE NEWS MEDIA

This is an oft-repeated lament. When big corporations began the takeover of television channels and their news divisions in the 1980s, they came with a slash-and-squeeze mindset that hasn't abated. No doubt you've heard it before, even from the mouths of major news anchors. Some unkind critics have detected hypocrisy in a situation where the industry's leading lights complain that cost-cutting is gutting their profession, while they negotiate ever larger salaries for themselves. In Chapter 6, the anchors talk about their salaries, and how several of them felt that a portion of their paychecks might better be spent on news gathering. (None of them, by the way, would reveal how much they earn.) And before I get accused of hypocrisy, let me say that I have not had a pay raise since 1992, when I was making a healthy six-figure salary. And if we are going to be really candid, I will confess that I have long said (to myself, not my agent) that I'd rather earn less and see the return of higher standards in my profession.

In 1986, when it looked as if Ted Turner might take over CBS (what a missed opportunity!), Lawrence Tisch of the Loews Corporation was brought in as a "white knight" to stave off the takeover. Why him—the worst bottom-fishing operator of all, a man better known for his ability to maximize his stake in businesses than for his nose for news and broadcasting? After he took control of the company, Tisch made a grand tour of the foreign news bureaus; at each stop the local bureau entertained him in the old CBS style (lavishly). But lavish was not Tisch's style, and when the Rome bureau chief held a reception for Tisch and brought in every stringer and handyman who had ever worked for the bureau, Tisch was horrified. I guess I didn't help things myself when I proudly told him that CBS staffed the London bureau like a firehouse, with correspondents and crews standing by ready to spring into action for any news emergency. That appalled him even more. Of course, Tisch didn't tell us his real thoughts at the time. Instead, he murmured sweet words about his commitment to news—and, above all, his intention not to cut the staff but to make better use of it. In the end, of course, he cut the staff.[5]

At least Jack Welch had the virtue of bluntness and candor when GE took over NBC in 1986. Wall Street worshipped the chairman of GE for his fanatical devotion to the bottom line. Welch ran his businesses ruthlessly to win, and like many other CEOs he defined winning as maximum profit with minimum possible outlay, and the highest payoff for shareholders. As simple as that. The news business, as a tiny part of the whole, got fed indiscriminately into the formula.

Lawrence Grossman, president of NBC at the time, hailed from a different school. He explains how in October 1987, when the stock market plunged, "Brokaw was talking about Black Monday and all of that. The next morning, I get a call from Jack Welch, who said, 'What do you guys think you are doing? You are killing this company. You are ruining our stock price.' I said, 'What are you talking about?' He said, 'You've got to get those guys of yours to stop talking about Black Monday.' I said, 'The fact is, it is the biggest drop since 1929.'

'But look what you are doing to the value of this company. My job is to keep the stock price up.'

I said, 'Jack, this conversation is not going out of my ear into anybody's because if anybody heard about this it would be disastrous.' We had a hell of a battle. There was just no understanding."

In Welch's book, *Jack: Straight from the Gut,* published the week the World Trade Center was destroyed, he complains that he and Grossman lived on "different planets." Grossman operated "under the theory that the networks should lose money while covering news in the name of journalistic integrity." Guess who won. Grossman now writes a column for the *Columbia Journalism Review,* and is one of the sharpest critics of the current state of American journalism, especially the decline of foreign news.

Most Americans who still remember the appalling industrial inefficiency and labor unrest of the 1970s believe, with some justification, in the CEO-imposed formula for streamlined business practices aimed at maximizing shareholder payouts. Yet there's also nothing new about companies whose rise in share value costs the public even more than the shareholders gain. After all, Halliburton's shares have hit massive highs since the Iraq War and President Bush's reelection, as have the shares of major defense companies. Yet faith in the profit-at-any-cost formula endures. The 1990s collapses of such hastily conglomerated, formula-run giants as Enron and Worldcom haven't changed the formula at all. The disasters are blamed on corrupt CEOs—not on the formula, though it seems to lead inexorably to outsourcing abroad, job losses at home, fewer benefits, and lower wages.

Perhaps that's as it should be, and we will all be richer for it; I'm not economist enough to render a verdict. But nobody seems to notice that, even by those ruthless principles, with the events of 9/11, the cutback of news output has proved costly for the very conglomerates that made those cutbacks in the first place—GE, Disney, Viacom, Time Warner et al. Who knows but that, with the kind of foreknowledge (and loud drumbeat) that a real news operation could have provided, all of us, including those conglomerates, might have avoided the disaster of 9/11. Nobody has done a proper study of how badly 9/11 and the ensuing conflicts affected their bottom line. The blow to tourism and the airlines alone certainly hurt Disney's theme park revenues for many months. GE's airline leasing, reinsurance, and other businesses surely sustained extensive damage. Equally, entertainment, celebrity and movies—Viacom's principal business—took a back seat for many months. And the values of these companies' shares must have taken a long-term hit.[6] Any conglomerate with a far-flung business empire across continents needs to know about instability and unrest in their market countries. Responsible CEOs need such information to hedge against disaster. Forget the national interest (as they did by news cutting); surely their own bottom line requires them to be more informed about events abroad than they can possibly be today.

They cut their own throats when they cut the news.

The pursuit of profit above public duty certainly has a lot to do with our failures as a profession. If you look for cause and effect, you needn't look too far from the above menu; and many critics, not least journalists themselves, have repeatedly made many of the same points. But even if you reversed the changes imposed by slavish adherence to market forces, you'd still be left to deal with other underlying and deep-seated problems that bedevil the news fraternity. The focus on profits simply made those things worse.

Having a news media that was free to do the job of providing the best and most important news, and to rendering it comprehensible and relevant, would have made this country less insular, better prepared, for the challenges it faces today. As it stands, recent developments—such as the advent of narrowcasting and Internet news—will make the job even harder. In the unbridled democracy of the World Wide Web, every outlandish, wacko point of view gets equal billing with the serious players. In 1980, 75 percent of the television sets in use were tuned in to one of the three evening news broadcasts, which acted as gatekeepers for the national consciousness. By 2003, their combined share of viewers had dropped to 40 percent, and it is still falling.[7] As the news audience increasingly fragments, with segments of the public turning to different media for only the news they want, the public is losing sight of the forest for the trees—and in the process it is growing ever easier for the government to manipulate our collective assumptions. (Witness the Bush administration's attempt to imply a connection between al Qaeda and Saddam Hussein: Once the seed was planted, you couldn't shake it in the public mind.)

In the future, then, it will be harder and harder to tell people what they need to know, even if the networks should reawaken to that duty. The eyeballs simply aren't in one place anymore. Obviously there can be benefits to getting one's news from multiple sources; others have made that case often enough that I won't bother to state the obvious again. There is another, not-so-obvious that does need saying: Our industry itself has too long suffered from a case of "groupthink," and the fragmentation of news sources may finally change that. Forget the divisive controversies over Vietnam and the current debates over Iraq. They are aberrations. Most of the time, in truth, most of the media take their cues from *the government* in deciding which foreign stories to cover. In the latter Clinton years, for example, when his Iraq policy stood at an impasse and American pilots patrolled the no-fly zones simply because the administration couldn't decide what else to do, the White House did not want to hear about Iraq. And the news media went along with it: Except for the occasional flare-up, few reports surfaced about the cat-and-mouse game America played with Saddam Hussein for ten years.

This kind of groupthink reduces all the news into a homogenous repetitive gray sludge. Even catastrophes and massacres become tiresome when Big News starts to drone on about them, often with no helpful warning beforehand, no context throughout, and endless mournful rehashing after the fact. When President Clinton had the gall to tour Africa apologizing publicly for ignoring that continent's travails—when a little White House leadership would clearly have helped far more a few years earlier, instantly raising Africa's profile in the media—the media gave the trip its adoring gaze of approval. Of course, the reverse is equally true: Had the media made an effort to cover developing events in Africa, the coverage might have shamed the White House into action. But as we know, recent American administrations have shown very little interest in trying to sort out that continent's problems. So the media go there rarely, except to cover the most horrible catastrophes. When the trouble began between the Hutus and the Tutsis in 1994, CBS sent me to Africa to report on the story in Rwanda. I filed one story and was pulled out by the foreign editor after seventy-two hours to cover another story in the Balkans. *Been there, done that.* Eight hundred thousand eventually died in that African genocide, but the media, the United Nations, and the Western governments all turned a blind eye. The overwhelming coverage came, as usual, too late.

Cutbacks, bottom-line fever, and CEO-mandated news criteria actually reinforce groupthink in mainstream news media in ways that can wildly distort the news. You can't get a more striking example than the amazingly mistaken election-day exit polling by the networks in 2004, which initially indicated pro-Kerry outcomes. Why were they so uniformly wrong? Because they all got together and pooled their resources to cut costs, sharing the same polling companies when a little competitive reporting might have kept the networks themselves on their toes.

This kind of herdlike laziness has infected the bloodstream of mainstream news organizations. It runs so deep, they don't even know it's there. No one gets fired for saying the obvious. Conventional wisdom dominates, and few news executives question received truths. I can tell you something about that, because I had a run-in with my bosses early in my career that I will never forget, or forgive.

In the days when I worked as Paris correspondent for CBS News, one of my neighbors was Sadegh Gotbzadeh, an elegant Iranian dissident who later became his country's foreign minister and was ultimately hanged by the Islamic fundamentalists he helped bring to power. Though he wore Gucci shoes and Pierre Cardin suits, Gotbzadeh somehow became close to Ayatollah Khomeini, and knew that Iran faced an imminent revolution. He convinced me that the Shah was in trouble. In October 1978, I went to Tehran with a television team, talked in private with the left-wing professors and right-wing clerics who held increasing sway over a growing student revolt, interviewed the few who dared speak more openly, had a few problems of my own with the Iranian police, and came back with a story that no one else believed—least of all the producers who ran the *CBS Evening News*.

I still have a faded copy of the script they would not air, and cannot resist quoting parts of it:

> The Shah's regime is one the United States has a keen interest in supporting. In the past twenty years, the U.S. has sold more than eighteen billion dollars in arms to the Shah. This, plus sales of technology, earns the United States two dollars for every dollar spent on Iranian oil. What the regime lacks is the support of its own people. The population's list of grievances is long. Opponents say corruption in the imperial court is almost unbelievable. Certainly, the wealth of the imperial family is hard to believe. Outside Tehran, the Shah's private foundation is building a multi-billion dollar new city for the well-to-do—allegedly with diverted petrodollars on land that was nationalized and then sold to the Shah's interests.

> . . .

> No Iranian can feel safe from arbitrary arrest and imprisonment by Savak, the secret police trained and organized by the CIA and the Israeli Mossad. As estimated 170,000 Iranians have been jailed for political reasons since the Shah assumed his dictatorial powers in 1953. Despite Savak's past record of torture, there is evidence that some American advisors still work for it.

> . . .

> As a conciliatory gesture, the Shah has now ordered the release of a thousand prisoners jailed for possessing banned books, or lesser crimes. Such gestures have not appeased the opposition to the Shah, which is a deep and wide as the country's attachment to the Shi'ite branch of Islam. Religion seems to be the one force that can rally the vast majority of the population. Except for a small communist element, the

loosely organized opponents of the Shah—who range from devout Muslims to old-line liberals and leftist intellectuals— have turned to the mosque as their only possible forum for political dissent.

If it were not for groupthink, CBS viewers—in those days a large portion of the American public—would have seen that story and heard the truth about a country the United States has still not come to terms with.[8] But my producers in New York had consistently read a different, more upbeat, version of events, in news magazines and on the wires, and could not believe their own correspondent's reporting from Iran. According to certain journalists who had received gifts from the imperial court, the Shah was a great reformer who sat firmly on his throne. Less than three months after I wrote my script, the Shah left Iran in disgrace.

The moral of that story is, simply, that everything old is new again: network news has always suffered from seriously bad habits, which the developments listed above only exacerbate. At least in those days CBS News actually *had* a Paris bureau, which happened to help me catch wind of behind-the-scenes realities in Iran; it also offered ample funding, which allowed me to hop over there to see for myself. But the ignorance and resistance to unexpected truths back at home base in New York has grown worse with fewer bureaus and correspondents. News bosses distracted by corporate wars do not excel at covering foreign ones. And what's worse: they don't believe anyone will notice or care.

CHAPTER FOUR

THE CULTURE
OF SPIN

We live in a time when, suddenly, it seems almost impossible to know the real facts about the most pivotal life-altering public events of our day. The more important the event, the murkier it gets. The invasion of Iraq: Why did President Bush really go in? Who was really responsible for the Abu Ghraib prison abuses? Who authorized the secret post 9/11 escape of high-level Saudis out of the country? Which of the Swift Boat veterans told the truth about Senator Kerry's Vietnam record? What about the battle over President Bush's National Guard documents—where does the truth lie there? Reality has never been so slippery, so seemingly impossible to nail down. And that's leaving aside anything that borders on conspiracy theory, or important foreign news events such as the Russian war in Chechnya. If we can't get to the bottom of our own affairs, what hope do we have of untangling messy foreign mysteries? I'm not talking about opinion, or what we feel about the facts—just the facts themselves. Facts come first, before we can hope to judge, say, the rights and wrongs of Donald Rumsfeld's war leadership, or which candidate to choose for president. For all the raucous crossfire of noise and reporting during the 2004 electoral season, Americans couldn't seem to reach first base when it came to the simple facts. We now inhabit a world so dizzy with "spin" that perception has all but obliterated fact.

The fault originates with the politicians, of course, but the blame must lie with the news media. Politicians spin the truth—that is what they do for a living. The news media's job is supposed to be unscrambling that spin, separating truth from lies. One of our most important jobs, actually. But it's just not working anymore. The public simply doesn't know what's going on much of the time. They don't know who to trust and what to believe. The one thing the public does seem to agree on more and more consistently, alas, is that the news media can't be fully trusted. According to a Gallup survey conducted on September 13–15, 2004, as many as 39 percent of those surveyed said they had "not very much" confidence in the media's accuracy and fairness, and 16 percent had "none at all." So when real facts do emerge, it's hard for people to recognize them as impartial and true, and even harder to allow the truth to change their own built-in biases.

To take one example: As a purely factual matter, America should know by now that Secretary of Defense Donald Rumsfeld chose to invade Iraq with far fewer troops than a preponderance of experts recommended—too few, as it turned out. This is a judgment that's been made by many top military voices. Even Ambassador Paul Bremer, the former U.S. official who governed Iraq after the invasion, has admitted that the United States "never" had enough troops on the ground to establish firm control of the country, directly contradicting assertions by the Pentagon and the president that the military had what it needed.[1] It follows that, as a result of his mistake, more American troops than necessary have lost their lives. It equally follows that the Iraqi insurrection has lasted much longer as a result.

In addition, fifty-three retired American diplomats signed a letter on May 4, 2004, saying that the Bush administration made a mess of the diplomacy around the war. As late as September 9, 2004, the *Financial Times,* in a story by correspondents James Drummond and Steven Negus, reported from Baghdad that "U.S. military officers in Baghdad have warned they cannot guarantee the security of the perimeter around the Green Zone, the headquarters of the Iraqi government and home to the U.S. and British Embassies, according to security company employees." Considering that the Green Zone represents the beating heart of the allied presence, the news from Iraq could not get worse. Yet interim Iraq Prime Minister Ayad Allawi claimed in his address to Congress on September 24, 2004, that "we are succeeding in Iraq." Contrary to his pronouncement, the facts are clear: The very figures who publicly advocated the invasion of Iraq have badly bungled their unilateral project. Yet, a large segment of America discounts or distrusts the evidence. President Bush campaigned for reelection as a strong war leader, and much of the country agreed. What is going on here?

One simple answer is that politicians and the media have conspired to infantilize, to dumb down, the American public. At heart, politicians don't believe that Americans can handle complex truths, and the news media, especially television news, basically agrees. Let's imagine a more grown-up, spin-free version of politics in the George W. Bush era. The president might begin by saying this to the public:

> This country is under threat. But not just here. I mean, the threat goes beyond attacks on our homeland. It's a gathering

threat to our access to oil worldwide. We've got to protect
those supplies from rivals like the Islamic fundamentalists or
Russia and China. You know, Russian and China signed a
strategic treaty in the 1990s to counter American power. But
even without that, I want to tell you that the demand for oil
will increase so much in the next twenty years because the
economies of China and India are expanding, that we might
not be able to compete. I don't believe we Americans can cut
back enough on oil consumption to make a difference. You
know, Russia owns a big chunk of the world's oil. The Muslims control another large chunk. Either they are going to
dictate whose economy grows at what rate, or we will continue to do so. Which choice do you prefer? I choose America because we are a democracy and we believe in free and
fair markets in the long term. Others don't. If we are to prevail, we have to guarantee our power and unhindered access
to oil markets in the short term. That means we have to reassert control over the Middle East. This isn't colonialism.
We will also bring huge benefits to Iraq. But we must install
pro-American democracies where we can, by force if necessary, or we face an unstable world and a poorer America. I
mean, you would have fewer SUVs. It would also mean elec-
tricity cuts, civil strife, inflation, high crime, lousy defense,
malnutrition, and the like. Are you ready for that, or are you
with me?

Had the president been so forthcoming, the media and the people would have been able to debate the choices in grown-up
fashion. Instead, the public was offered one shifty rationale
after another for the invasion of Iraq: first the prospect that
Iraq had weapons of mass destruction (WMD), then the urgency of the war on terror, then the policy of "regime change,"
then the noble goal of bringing democracy to the Mideast.
In truth, we *still* don't know why we're in Iraq. That's why

Americans seem so unsure why, or whether, we should endure the hardship this war entails. In fact, many thinking Americans don't understand why we're not being asked to endure any sacrifices at home, with the economy awash in debt. Regardless of what it thought of John Kerry, though, as of this writing the public still finds President Bush credible as a war leader in the polls. Between September and mid-October 2004, a Rasmussen Report poll found that between 42 and 44 percent of people continued to support his leadership in Iraq. This, in the face of continuous bad news from Iraq and criticism in the press. How is that possible?

One possible answer is that the public now believes the media to be utterly politicized and partisan—caught up in its own spin, as it were. This is not the first time in recent decades that the news media and public opinion have been at odds. From the Nixon through the Carter administrations, the press had the upper hand. But all that changed with Ronald Reagan, the Teflon president, who consistently out-communicated the media, and grew in popularity the more he was criticized by the press. Richard Nixon may have hated the press passionately, but it was Reagan who first institutionalized scorn for journalists by cherry-picking the correspondents he allowed into White House briefings, or by simply not calling on those who dared ask provocative questions. The news outlets, anxious to keep their seats at the briefings, went along with it. It was this era that saw the birth of the "exclusive" interview—the Barbara Walters-style therapeutic talkathon in which the interviewee (often a politician) agonized over one soft, fuzzy, cozy question after another. Interviews of this kind signaled the triumph of chat show values over news values and, more insidiously, the subliminal moment when star network interviewers began to undermine their news colleagues by turning politicians into icons. Meanwhile, in the case of Ronald Reagan, real journalists shot themselves in the foot with knee-jerk leftist critiques of a popular president who was busy winning the Cold War—a journalistic mistake that has hobbled us ever since.

Similarly, President Clinton's popularity suffered little during the Monica Lewinsky scandals and impeachment proceedings. Rightly or wrongly, the public learned to read a degree of spin into the news media's oppositional posture; one could see the same effect with President Bush. Yet, even if you combine all the anti-Bush or antiwar coverage in the United States and double it, the result is nothing compared to the attacks that can be found regularly in the European or Middle Eastern media. Most foreign news channels regard American reporting of foreign affairs as deeply insular and self-serving, and with some reason: American television, for example, almost never shows scenes of Iraqi victims being killed by American troops, or blown up by helicopters, a standard spectacle on Al Jazeera and various European channels. Americans, in their current mood, would probably bridle at such spectacles and deem them to be vulgar anti-Bush, antiwar, even anti-American propaganda. So instead Americans get a partial view of a partial view—and even that they often choose to discount. So spin has triumphed in the worst possible way, by confusing the public's very ability or even inclination to recognize the truth. And historically this comes, at the worst possible time. In such an environment, conspiracy theories gain traction; indeed, it can even help foster a breeding ground for true conspiracies at the highest level. And while we argue among ourselves, our enemies continue to proliferate abroad.

The triumph of spin is largely the news media's own fault. Certainly the industry got caught in a pincer from both flanks, politicians on the one hand and owners on the other. But we took sides with them, and allowed them to influence our judgment; indeed they became part of our business and we theirs. On the political front, too many journalists became political mouthpieces while remaining journalists—and others simply took the King's shilling, as it were, and went to work officially for politicians. The practice goes back a long way. The Nixon White House, for example, hired a number of reporters, including Ray Price (from the now defunct *New York Herald*), Pat Buchanan, and William Safire. Their functions, on the whole, stayed within honorable boundaries, as did their conduct—they knew not to undermine the codes of their alma mater, the Fourth Estate.

During the Clinton era, though, hacks in and out of the White House's employ increasingly became political hit men, and the line began to blur in earnest. Former *Washington Post* and *New Republic* reporter Sidney Blumenthal joined the White House as a senior aide. He took on a kind of attack-dog role for his masters, drawing on professional contacts and old friendships to leak and smear; the anti-Clintonites took to calling him "Sid Vicious." Prominent figures in journalism such as Geraldo Rivera and Joe Conason took sides openly as partisan advocates for Clinton. Whereas someone like Rush Limbaugh never pretended to be anything other than a partisan pundit, both Geraldo and Conason had found earlier fame as noisy investigative, anti-establishment, reporters. During the Clinton years, Geraldo was reincarnated as a nightly apologist for the administration on his own political chat show for CNBC. Conason, as his frequent guest, authored the book *The Hunting of the President,* which peddled the vast right-wing conspiracy theory. (Geraldo's Fox News gig came later.) Meanwhile, the *New York Times Magazine* published a famous article entitled "The Clinton Haters," suggesting that those who criticized Bill Clinton too much did so out of some irrational or visceral personal antipathy, and that they conspired to use the news media as their tool—in other words, that they were "nutters" with powerful media allies. (The concept endured into the Bush era with the advent of "Bush-Bashers.") You could be forgiven for thinking that parts of the news media had transformed into Lenin-era blocs: the collaborators, the useful idiots, and the disloyal opposition. No doubt this is the kind of thing that the modern-day Lenin, Vladimir Putin, had in mind when he said, "the press is not an institution, it's an instrument."[2]

Don't suppose for a moment that things got better under George W. Bush, or that such dubious conflicts of interest applied only to presidential reporting. The public can see perfectly clearly that on many fronts, and for many often hidden reasons, the press cannot or will not reveal various faces of the truth. The glaring issue of corporate ownership of news media, and the conflicts that come with it, get raised often—and just as often get dismissed.

Spin operates in many insidious ways; it even gets into our public anti-spin machinery. Apparently, even the blue-ribbon 9/11 Commission was not immune, having convened reluctantly only after continuous public pressure came from 9/11 widows who were loudly demanding answers. In his recent book *Cover Up: What the Government Is Still Hiding About the War on Terror,* Peter Lance offers astonishing and well-documented details of continuing spin and damage control by the FBI and other agencies on perhaps the single most important event in our history since World War II. If we can't investigate even this without the taint of corruption—and if the media fails to tell us how and why—then things are bleak indeed. As Lance remarks in the book, "If the Commission had had more time, better funding, and more objective staff members—and had they been less influenced by election-year politics—the final report of the Commission might have offered a more honest rendition of the truth."[3]

Lance's book meticulously documents how the 9/11 Commission—by its very structure, its appointed personnel, the weirdly limited scope of its mission—operated as a vast act of spin, apparently in order to bring the matter to a swift and palatable close. No doubt putting the past behind us was a worthy enough sentiment at a time when the country needed to steel itself for the present and future. But to do so, the country also needed to know what exactly happened—not a version carefully spun to soothe our souls or benefit political agendas, however worthy. Of the seventy-five staff members acknowledged on the web site of the Commission, thirty-two were employees of either the agencies being investigated or the Congressional oversight committees whose failures allowed 9/11 to happen. Here again, the public apparently couldn't be trusted with a fully complex, grownup presentation of the truth. As one of the 9/11 widows is quoted as saying, "In the end, you have to ask yourself which is worse, the idea that the nation's leaders were involved in every detail and still couldn't keep [9/11] from happening, or that they were AWOL? After all this time, we still don't have the full truth from the 9/11 Commission." Lance's book is a painstakingly documented chronicle of good (transparent) and bad (murky) in the Commission's work, but the bad—the oversights and cover-ups—really shake one's faith. Above all, the book serves as a loud cry of frustration that so much spin goes undetected, so many worrisome facts are left to lie there unexplored. Of the many alarming omissions in the 9/11 Commission's work that he lays out, here are a few:

- On the morning of 9/11, three separate war-game exercises were in progress—including one that envisioned a plane crashing into a government building. (Despite claims by National Security Advisor Condoleezza Rice and others that no one imagined such a thing.) Lance also reports that two F-16s were eight minutes from Manhattan, but the FAA failed to contact them. Why do these exercises go almost unmentioned in the 9/11 Commission Report?
- How did lead hijacker Mohammed Atta get a pass allowing him access to a restricted area of Logan Airport prior to his hijacking of AA Flight 11?
- Why did it take the FAA eighteen minutes to report the first hijacking to NORAD—a critical delay that hampered the government's ability to respond effectively? And why does the gap go almost unmentioned in the Commission's final report?
- According to the *Washington Post* and the Israeli newspaper *Haaretz,* at least two workers at the research and development offices of Odigo, Inc., near Tel Aviv, received warnings of an imminent attack on New York City two hours before the first plane hit the Twin Towers. The broadcast warning did not mention the World Trade Center. The company informed the FBI immediately after the attack began. Odigo, an Israeli-owned instant messaging company, has its headquarters two blocks from the WTC. The Commission refused to probe the matter.[4]

■ Some three hundred Saudi nationals were allowed to flee the United States in the days immediately after 9/11, many with special permission. The Commission addresses the facts only partially and incorrectly, saying that the Saudis mostly left when commercial flights resumed or only after being fully interrogated. In fact, of the three hundred-odd Saudis who left, only thirty were questioned. Why?

This is a chapter about spin, but, in the interests of impartiality, let's not forget what we've already said in previous chapters about how the media more or less gave the Clinton White House a free ride in matters of national security, despite the incompetence it demonstrated in fighting the terror threat worldwide. That failure helped pave the way for the 9/11 horror. But the Bush administration was running things when 9/11 happened, and it was they, too, who took us into Iraq. It is in the Bush era that the reign of spin has achieved unparalleled supremacy. Perhaps a new Tom Wolfe or Norman Mailer will turn up to record for history the bizarre sensation of what the Bush era felt like: a time when deceit and delusion so addled the public faculties that we became unable to locate reality. President Bush could scarcely point to a single successful policy by the end of his first term, yet the spin skills of his team—led by Karl Rove—overcame all, savagely smearing anyone who stood in the way. Hard not to resort to smear, perhaps, when defending a tenure in which a stream of top officials left, either for incompetence—such as George Tenet— or for disgust with the incompetence around them, such as Paul O'Neill, Richard Clarke, and Lawrence B. Lindsey.

Larry Lindsey, the president's former chief economist, had to go for criticizing Bush spending. Treasury Secretary Paul

O'Neill and anti-terror czar Richard Clarke both authored books fiercely critical of the president and his *a priori* plans to invade Iraq; both were made to look like embittered egomaniacs trying to sell their books. But they got off lightly. The Democrat who opposed Bush for reelection, John Kerry, suffered the *Unfit for Command* campaign by a group calling itself "Swift Boat Veterans for Truth." This was nothing new, of course, considering the way Karl Rove had disposed of Senator John McCain during the Republican nomination race in 2000 with rumors that McCain might be unstable precisely due to his war heroism. In fact, Karl Rove's vicious tactics go back a very long way: An October 2004 *Atlantic Monthly* article analyzing Bush-Rove tactics recalled the campaign manager's early pre-Bush triumph against an Alabama Supreme Court judge named Mark Kennedy who was seeking reelection. Justice Kennedy had worked on many child welfare projects. The article quotes a Rove staffer as saying that "some within the [Rove] camp initiated a whisper campaign that Kennedy was a pedophile." Rove's tactics succeeded: Judge Kennedy and family were so appalled that Kennedy withdrew from the race.

Good spin and efficient news media work in exactly inverse ratio to each other. An effective press prevents successful spin. The Bush White House successfully confused the public because the news media failed badly. Here is a list of massive Bush administration spin that succeeded, against all common sense, in getting past our defenses.

- National Security Adviser Condoleezza Rice publicly defended the Bush administration's failure to avert 9/11 by pleading ignorance, even though the CIA's then-director, George Tenet, testified officially that "the system was blinking red" not two weeks before the attacks. (Despite these oversights, President Bush elevated Rice to the position of secretary of state in his second term.)

- When Hamid Karzai's interim government took over, the Afghanistan war was treated as over, and the focus shifted to Iraq. Then, once our attention was diverted, the warlords slowly resumed control of Afghanistan. The opium trade multiplied. And bin Laden dropped further and further out of sight.

- The administration's once-fanciful efforts to conflate the war on terror with the war in Iraq were eventually rendered legitimate—not because Saddam was sponsoring terrorism (the administration never managed to present convincing evidence of that) but because the American presence in Iraq after Saddam's overthrow became a breeding ground for terrorism.

- The allies kept no record of Iraqi casualties during the war or in the postwar conflict. How many innocents were being killed by American action and how many by terrorists? Were we winning hearts and minds? We had no way of knowing.[5]

- Despite saying of the Abu Ghraib prison abuses that "I am accountable for them and I take full responsibility," Donald Rumsfeld retained his post, raising a question central to the Bush administration: What does "I take full responsibility" mean?

- Who was really responsible for the fact that only 10 percent of the Humvees that were sent to Iraq were armored, which led to many postwar American troop casualties? At the Republican National Convention, Georgia Senator Zell Miller blamed the problem on John Kerry for his military cost-cutting votes as a senator, yet surely the Bush (and Clinton) administrations should shoulder far more of the blame than one easy-target senator.

- Nobody noticed that the crucial business of allied propaganda within Iraq and in the Arab world failed completely for a full year. SAIC, the California company chosen to run Voice of Iraq radio and a national newspaper, had no previous media experience—but plenty of ex-military bigwigs on its board. Inside Iraq, they convinced no one that the allied cause was just. Their patrons, the Department of Defense, finally put a "stop work" order on them late in 2003.[6] The news media totally missed the issue.

- In his reelection campaign, for obvious reasons, President Bush virtually stopped making any reference to bin Laden—until the terrorist released a video just before the election. (Bush also stopped making reference to the developing North Korean and Iranian nuclear threats.)

- Despite the fact that their use of humiliation showed sophisticated knowledge of local Arab taboos, we don't yet know who taught the Abu Ghraib prison guards to use their barbaric interrogation techniques.

- By mid-2004, only 2 percent of the $18.4 billion authorized the previous October by Congress for aid to Iraq had been spent.[7] The money simply wasn't getting there. Why not? Where was it?

- According to Saddam Hussein's appointed lawyer, Giovanni di Stefano, a Gallup poll conducted in mid-2004 showed that 42 percent of Iraqis wanted Saddam back as leader. The poll went virtually unreported in the U.S. media.

■ As of this writing, the United States still hasn't reinforced Iraq's borders with troops enough to monitor infiltration by outsiders—outsiders whom it blamed for much of the insurgency.

Here, then, was a sitting American president running for reelection, and winning—despite the long list of problems he should have been made to answer for. George W. Bush clearly conducted his spin management far better than his foreign military ventures. None of these glaring oversights would have existed if the news media were doing its job properly. Spin makes journalists lazy, and lazy journalists allow spin to succeed. When various interest groups leak "facts" clandestinely to their favorite reporters, reporters get dependent and don't do their skeptical homework, because they're too busy buddying up their sources.

Often the sources suit the journalists' political bias in the first place. Two glaring examples of just this have marred the profession's reputation in recent months: the strident advocacy of the Iraq invasion by the *New York Times*'s Judith Miller, and Dan Rather's CBS *60 Minutes* debacle over the handling of the Bush National Guard documents. In the Judith Miller case, her overcommitted position became exposed only after her main source, Ahmed Chalabi, was discredited. A longtime leader of Iraqi exile groups, Chalabi had sold Miller—and the Bush White House—a misleading picture of an Iraq full of WMD and an Iraqi people ready to rise up in support of American troops. After the invasion, when neither notion proved correct, Chalabi was hit with accusations that he'd been working for the Iranians all along. Though he denied the charge, he was then publicly quoted as saying that, despite the

Iraqi resistance and the disappearing WMD, he had nevertheless been successful: He'd managed to get the United States to
invade. Suddenly, Judith Miller's unquestioning use of Chalabi
information began to look very shabby indeed.

In the case of Dan Rather, the veteran anchor had to admit
authenticity problems in documents that threw doubts on
President Bush's National Guard service. CBS had rushed the
story onto the air without fully verifying the documents, which
turned out to be fake. Result? President Bush got a free pass on
his questionable National Guard record—and on much else.
Suddenly, Bush apologists and the Fox News Channel could
crow noisily that they'd been right all along—that any news
that shone a critical light on the Bush administration's performance was a function of leftish bias, not of hard fact. (This is
particularly rich coming from Fox, a network that specializes
in endless discussion and commentary and right-wing spin—
and almost no original fact-finding.) As it stands, these days
the networks barely have enough hard news manpower to go
out and uncover stories unaided. Not surprisingly, the dis-
pelling of spin much of the time begins on Internet blogs (as
happened with the Rather case), not on the network news.

The American news media's coziness with power looks
even starker from the perspective of other democracies, where
some news channels still assume an adversarial or at least
skeptical role. Sometimes this gets them in trouble and opens
the door to Dan Rather-like problems, as happened between
the BBC and Prime Minister Tony Blair. When BBC reporter
Andrew Gilligan reported that the prime minister's office had
"sexed up" the public dossier on Saddam Hussein's weapons
of mass destruction, the thrust of Gilligan's report was correct. But when it emerged that he may have overstated his
case, Gilligan resigned his job under pressure from the govern-

ment, as did the chairman and director general of the BBC. On the whole, though, the public in the United Kingdom and in Europe generally expects journalists to pressure their politicians and leaders mercilessly.

An illustration of how we differ from our European counterparts occurred when President Bush traveled through Ireland on June 25, 2004, and faced a hardnosed interview by Carole Coleman on Irish TV. Coleman challenged Bush's stock non-answers, and interrupted him several times in an effort to get him to say something meaningful. The encounter caused an uproar from Bush spokesmen and apologists, not least because the president clearly had grown unused to such relentless questioning—which is par for the course in much of Europe. The incident demonstrated how American presidents have been able to "manage" interviews ahead of time for so long that they can't handle the real thing. The White House's outrage appeared even odder, considering that the Irish station had submitted all the questions to White House handlers ahead of time.

So much for presidential spin. There are many other insidious kinds, and they have an equally corrupting effect on our profession. Parent corporations, advertisers, and commercial interests operate invisible levers over the news a great deal of the time, but for obvious reasons the public rarely hears about such influence. Any employee who has witnessed a direct intervention from upstairs to squelch a story generally stays quiet. If the intervening power is so influential as to be successful, no lone employee will dare take them on. Several journalists who, on condition of anonymity, described instances where documentaries or investigative segments were pulled or softened, ultimately refused to participate in this book, for fear of being identified and blacklisted.

One glaring public example does exist, of course, and many people know about it, though most people probably regard it as an exception: the case of *60 Minutes* and the cigarette industry, which was later made into the movie *The Insider.* Mike Wallace and *60 Minutes* had prepared a story that detailed devastating allegations against the nation's third largest tobacco company. The CBS management, which was about to enter a $5.4 billion merger with Westinghouse, killed the story rather than face a likely multibillion dollar lawsuit from the tobacco company. Ironically, there was a silver lining within the cloud of cigarette smoke: Thanks to CBS's decision, the allegations by a former vice president of research and development at Brown and Williamson Tobacco Corporation captured continuing front-page coverage in the nation's press; indeed, the leaks about his charges probably got more sustained notice than the broadcast itself would have. They focused public attention on allegations that B&W squelched research on "safer" cigarettes; altered documents to remove damaging references to the "safe cigarette" project; used an additive known to cause cancer in laboratory animals in its pipe tobacco; and in testimony by its chief executive, lied to Congress about the addictive qualities of tobacco.

Most people probably consider this incident an exception, and in some ways, it was a relatively rare event—but only because direct intervention took place. Usually, journalists are savvy enough not to incite confrontation: They self-censor from the get-go. Sometimes journalists themselves ally with outside forces to distort or spin news, not necessarily for bribes but out of conviction, political bias, personal friendships, or ethnic solidarity. The last is a particularly worrisome trend, at a time when immigrants make up an increasing percentage of the population. Any time there's enough money to finance a lobby, it inevitably results in efforts to influence media coverage overtly and covertly. No one ever mentions the influence of ethnic lobbies or affiliations on American media in general—except in the case of Israel. There the influence appeared to have grown so glaring over so many years that a backlash set in: As far back as the 1982 Israeli invasion of Lebanon, Thomas Friedman complained that the *New York Times* had taken out the word "indiscriminate" from his phrase "indiscriminate bombing" by the Israelis. This particular concern seems to have reached something more like equilibrium in recent years: Correspondents of Jewish origin for mainstream news outlets now often bend over backwards to appear impartial.

But the influence is still there on many levels, on behalf not just of Israel but of any organized ethnic minority with an ax to grind in foreign affairs. Most Americans don't know, for instance, that a large Armenian community thrives in Syria, where they have lived in relative safety for nearly a century. Armenians also live in relative harmony in Iran. Both those countries are at daggers drawn with Israel. In the United States, Armenian and Jewish notions of what constitutes bias or impartiality in Middle Eastern reporting might, of necessity, differ. Journalists with ties to either region might likely have entirely opposing views of various events in the Middle East. Both groups can invoke their own tragic ethnic histories when their interests face too much criticism. Most Americans couldn't begin to detect such arcane levels of spin and counterspin in foreign reporting; to do so requires an exceedingly finely tuned sense for news nuance, and a very precise knowledge of foreign affairs.

Here's an example of preventive spin, one that combines both ethnic and corporate influence on a very important news item. On the day of 9/11, an old lady looking out of her window curtains at the New Jersey waterfront noticed a white van surrounded by excited young folk who were videotaping the burning towers and high-fiving each other. She called the police and gave them the van's number plate details, and the police stopped the van on the road and collared its occupants. They turned out to be Israelis. The incident eventually made it onto the public record in various news reports. At ABC News they decided, with some courage, to pursue the story—I say courage because it doesn't take much to be accused of anti-Semitism in any negative reporting about Israel, and the implications of this story were doubtless highly inflammatory. But the incident genuinely happened. Should the journalists have self-censored, knowing the outcry that might result? Other networks apparently passed on the story. Why were those figures videotaping and making celebratory gestures? Why were they there in the first place? Did they know anything ahead of time—and, if so, had they communicated what they knew to U.S. authorities? Had it been just one more warning that intelligence agencies couldn't get the Bush administration to heed?

The story raised all these issues—but no one could answer them, because the Israelis, by now under arrest, weren't talking. ABC News interviewed both the old lady and the police and prepared the segment for later transmission. Suddenly, however, word came down from ABC's parent company, Disney, that the story was too inflammatory in its current form and had to be altered. "Softened" is the word used by the ABC inside source on this murky tale. The story that ABC News eventually ran on its evening news and on *20/20* with Barbara Walters on June 21, 2002, suggested that the arrested men may have been "part of an Israeli operation aimed at monitoring radical Islamic charities that support groups like Hamas." Maybe—but if so, why were they videotaping the destruction of the towers and reacting with apparent joy? In the end, the Israeli embassy in Washington denied that they were part of a spy ring, and the arrested men, who were questioned for weeks by law enforcement officials, were eventually released and allowed to leave the country. No one, in officialdom or in the media, subsequently gave a coherent explanation of the events. In October 2004, the "white van" Israelis filed a multimillion-dollar suit against the Justice Department for illegal arrests and torture. Was that, too, a public act of spin? After all, if the Israelis are so outraged, why don't they sue the news outlets that originally carried the story?

What are we to make of all this? Even today, anyone relating the known events surrounding the white van incident—precious few facts are extant—must painstakingly and correctly hedge them with weighty disclaimers, because the story seems to reek of conspiracy theory. Is one suggesting that Israel perpetrated the 9/11 attacks? In describing these events, is one giving credence to all the Islamist canards about no Jews having died, or to the theory that inside forces planned 9/11 as a trigger to launch a crusade against Islam? You get the point. All of which raises the more fundamental question: Should the news media therefore have ignored the entire story because no one could get at the real explanation? The point—and here comes the spin—is that we still don't know what the white van incident really means, and chances are that we never will: The incident has been effectively fudged, and what once was an intriguing lead has instead become just another slippery piece of unfathomable reality.

One might, though, arrive at a reasonably plausible hypothesis. To begin with, various media organs—from *Le Monde* to Fox News to the online magazine *Salon*—reported that, in the summer of 2001, U.S. officials deported more than 120 Israelis as spies, many of whom were disguised as art students around the United States. Furthermore, after 9/11 numerous media reports emerged that the Israelis had warned American authorities more than once, in the preceding weeks of a major impending assault on the United States, and of specific terrorists living in the United States. Some names turned out to belong to the 9/11 hijackers. The reports appeared in media organs including the London *Daily Telegraph* (9/17/01), *Los Angeles Times* (9/20/01), *Ottawa Citizen* (9/17/01), *Der Spiegel* (10/1/02), BBC (10/2/02) and others.[8]

So what does all this mean? Here's a hypothesis: The Israeli spies had gathered enough information to warn the United States in a general way of the impending threat—and, as usual, officials ignored the warning. The white-van Israelis were congratulating each other because they'd guessed correctly at the WTC as the target. Having been proved right, they felt vindicated. The police interrogated them long enough to realize that their story would severely embarrass the Bush administration, so they released them. The Israeli government naturally wouldn't want to embarrass President Bush, so they refused to comment, even to save face. And nobody in the media has managed to put it all together. Spin wins. America loses.

On the other end of the spectrum from this plausible case of Israeli spin, we find the murky presence and influence of another longtime American ally: Saudi Arabia. Israel and the Saudis are comparable on very few grounds but one: their mastery of spin. Both countries exert a disproportionate amount of influence on how Americans see events in the Middle East and other parts of the world—indeed on American foreign policy as a whole. The Saudis, though, operate almost entirely below public visibility, deploying vast amounts of petrodollars in

Washington, D.C., backrooms, among oil industry circles in the United States and in American universities. The Saudis have also acted for years as clandestine proxy financiers for U.S. foreign policy objectives. In the 1980s, they helped President Reagan dodge Congressional interference by supplying funds directly to the Nicaraguan Contras. From the 1970s onward, they helped the U.S. counter communist ideas by funding *madrassas* around the Muslim world at a time when it made sense, when pro-Soviet propaganda dominated the region—and that was even before the Afghans' ideological gearing up against the Soviets. Remember the BCCI bank scandal in the early 1990s? Gulf and Saudi money underpinned the bank, which funneled funds to Islamic groups fighting the Soviets—all of which was allowed to unravel once the Soviets withdrew.

The Saudis certainly have powerful friends in Washington, but nobody knows how much direct influence they really exert over the media. Their form of influence turns into a form of invisible spin as it filters down through protective bureaucratic layers of "friends" on the payroll, who run flak for them quietly. You will not see any news pundits, politicians, or prominent citizens stand up proudly and declare, as many do with Israel, that they are strong supporters of Saudi Arabia. Yet neither will you see much on network news about the influence of Saudi money in Washington—which is a real phenomenon indeed. Various books published in the wake of 9/11 have detailed Saudi clout in American corridors of power, from ex-CIA agent Robert Baer's *Sleeping with the Enemy* to Craig Unger's *House of Bush, House of Saud* (which claims that the Bush family made $1.4 billion from the Saudis over the years). Yet there's still a great deal we don't know.

What we do know is that, since the 1990s, Saudi Arabia has become the leading hotbed of anti-American Islamist radicalism, with the help of some top Saudi royalty; that fifteen of the nineteen 9/11 hijackers hailed from Saudi Arabia; and that nearly three hundred elite Saudis flew out of American airspace unhindered soon after 9/11, many with special permission, some with apparent connections to al Qaeda. A great deal of the mystery centers around private flights said to have operated through U.S. airspace soon after 9/11, carrying top Saudis, at a time when the entire nation's civilian aviation was mostly grounded—or so the allegation goes. As Michael Moore's movie *Fahrenheit 9/11* and Craig Unger's book (and his web site, www.houseofbush.com) allege, one such flight consisted mainly of bin Laden family members. In rebuttal, FBI officials and others have uniformly resorted to spin, saying that no evidence exists of flights leaving the United States during the flight ban. But they don't explain the flights *within* the country. Nor do they explain why, if it was all routine and legal, the exodus required permission from someone very high up in the Bush administration. Thus far, only Richard Clarke in the administration admits to giving his approval to the flights, but he would hardly have dared make that decision on his own. And here's where the spin comes in: Both the Saudis and the Bush administration have gotten away with the fudging. Despite the 9/11 Commission's (incompetent) probe into the matter, despite the Bush backers' spinning attempts to saddle Richard Clarke with the full responsibility, we still don't know who okayed those flights, on whose authority, and why. And we don't know why anyone should try to fudge the entire issue. We do know that the Saudi royal family fears a Shi'ite-dominated democratic government in Iraq based on the majority Shi'ite population: In the wake of the American counterinsurgency operation against Sunni rebels in Fallujah (November 2004), the Saudi rulers allowed twenty-six prominent Saudi religious scholars to issue a call to arms urging Iraqis to resist the U.S. occupation. The Bush administration has said nothing on the matter, and the media has largely followed suit.

How is it that none of these issues are brought up in White House press briefings, where—in theory, at least—an army of correspondents can confront officials in a captive space with the country looking on? Answer: spin reigns there, as much as anywhere. Most people beyond the Beltway are unaware of how efficiently the White House controls the Washington media. One media insider—who has covered the White House for years, but prefers to remain anonymous because he wants to continue to cover the White House—describes the process this way:

> The Bush administration certainly plays favorites, as have the other administrations I've covered [Reagan and Clinton]. They don't shut us out; any idiot with a White House Press pass (and there are some certifiable cases) can come to the press secretary's daily briefing and ask whatever off-the-wall question he or she wishes. But the answers in that venue are usually anodyne. The policy line is repeated ad nauseam, even when it is contradicted by the obvious facts—as with the situation on the ground in Iraq. And even the daily news briefings can be manipulated. Reporters for the wires, networks and major papers, whose assigned seats are all in the first several rows, will sometimes get into a sustained colloquy with, or engage in serial interruptions of, the press secretary. But all the person on the podium need do to escape is look out into the crowd and call on a reporter whose question or area of interest was guaranteed to change the topic—someone from *The Times of India* or *Oil Daily,* to name two of the regulars. The querulous or the critical can be heard, but usually not at length.

As my colleague notes, the ritual of press room briefings is only part of the prickly relationship between reporters and the White House. "The question of access to senior administration officials and policymakers bedevils reporters in any administration, because the only access to those decision makers is by phone. They return the calls of reporters they know or like, or in whose publications they want information to appear (usually sourced to 'an administration official,' rather than by name)." Thus, in any administration—even the current one, with its well-known antipathy to the so-called liberal media elite—"it's easier to get a call returned if you work for the *New York Times* or the *Washington Post* than the *Toledo Blade.*"

"That said," he continues, "Bush administration officials, like those in previous administrations, may freeze out individual reporters whose work has annoyed them." Among the reporters who've received this treatment, he mentions the *Washington Post*'s Dana Milbank, whom he characterizes as "relentlessly" critical of the administration. "But the offenders usually spend only a limited amount of time in purdah," he observes, "and eventually rejoin the club. For any major news organization that has many people covering the major beats, it's not that important. But if you are a one-person Washington bureau for your paper, it certainly can be a big problem."

When it comes to network reporters, on the other hand, the White House has proven to be as ratings-conscious as the media executives. "The networks," my colleague notes, "are seen in relation to their ratings, and the personalities of their anchors. For example, the White House will often give NBC's *Today* show the live appearance of an administration guest, and force the other morning shows to pre-tape. Or they will give *Today* an exclusive, [because] it has by far the biggest morning ratings. It will sometimes make it clear that if there's to be an interview with, for example, the First Lady, one anchor might be favored over others as the interviewer. Both the White House and the networks keep careful track of which officials have been on which programs. Network interviews with the president are the ultimate reward—and they are also usually apportioned on a rotating basis, except when they're not. CBS has not gotten one lately—presumably because the president and his family don't care for Dan Rather."

In fact, although he affects a jokey camaraderie with the White House press corps, President Bush doesn't trust the media—as evidenced by his avoidance of solo press conferences. His distrust of the press permeates the White House; Vice President Cheney, for example, refuses to take *New York Times* reporters on his trips.

Too many Americans believe that spin amounts merely to the harmless he-said-she-said babble of opinion that marks any democracy. The truth is that an environment of untrammeled spin can damage us deeply. What if, amid the flurry of too-clever debating points, the truth never comes out? What if that truth, or its absence, threatens to destroy us? What if outside forces can manipulate our democratic decisions simply by deploying masters of spin among our newsmen and leaders?

By the time of the 2004 election, the administration spin had grown so thick in the air that even Republicans began to question it. The situation today comes dangerously close to the process of news via rumor that characterizes the *souks* and bazaars of less-advanced societies. The shrewdest rumorists can destroy lives and silence honest voices and wash away the truth, and along the way the populace becomes utterly confused, unable to separate conspiracy from fact. Americans are being served by a news media so beset by spin, from within and without, that we've lost all sense of what objective truth feels or sounds like. Spin acts as the cutting edge of the dumbing-down process that the rest of the entertainment media daily peddles: the substitution of fantasy for reality, and the conviction that the public cannot take too much truth—indeed is bored by it, especially in its most complex forms.

There's no doubt that politicians, power groups, and advertisers benefit from citizens who dutifully follow their leaders' instructions and go shopping in times of trouble. The citizens themselves, however, merely get fleeced.

CHAPTER FIVE

WHAT THE REST OF THE WORLD SEES

I n backward or totalitarian countries, official public real- ity is often a vast fiction fed to a miserable populace by rigidly controlled media. Usually, the fiction grows threadbare and absurdly bogus over time—visibly so to every- one from inside or outside the country. In his memoir, my old colleague Garrick Utley from NBC News tells a poignant story of covering the Soviet Union's sixtieth anniversary pa- rade in 1977.[1] After the usual tanks and missiles and troops rolled up Red Square for hours on end, he notes, a massive fireworks display took place. Sadly, low clouds obscured the starry bursts—so the producers simply added them into the video in the studio and the commentator extolled their bril- liance. As Utley notes, "the reality represented to the viewers was not what was, but what was supposed to be." Yet he also contends that "that sort of manipulation would not survive in the new information and media world." Well, here we are living in the brave new media age. What would you say—was he right? Perhaps such a blatant case of manipulation would have been exposed, but with today's technology there are plenty of other, more sophisticated brands of deceit that have replaced it. In fact, despite the access to infinite sources of information, we are surely witnessing the consistent triumph of spin over reality in our own country and elsewhere. It turns out the self-evident truth we believed in all along, that free societies get better information—or that plentiful information frees societies—isn't so simply axiomatic after all. The real world appears to work a lot more subtly than that.

Our old faith would suggest that truth triumphs over fiction in an open society because the public knows the difference. But what if, in an apparently competitive media system, the public still only gets inadequate or broadly slanted news? Is that even possible? If not, how does one explain the enormous divergence between European and American reporting on Iraq—a matter of not just opposing beliefs, but starkly opposed "factual" reporting? How to explain, for that matter, the reporting of Al Jazeera and Al Arabiya? Either they are biased or we are.

But they can't be making *everything* up. Take the case of Iraq: all the wounded children, the accidentally killed mothers, the homeless, the workless, the understaffed hospitals, the bad water, the sheer rage and hopelessness of many caught in the crossfire. We don't see much of that on the news here in America. But everyone else in the world does. It turns out that we're as resistant to certain kinds of truth as totalitarian countries—we who pride ourselves on our free flow of information! We certainly see a lot of burnt-out Humvees and bomb debris footage, but little else—except for the storm over Abu Ghraib, but that passed away soon enough.

Conservative media critics will tell you that a lot is going well in Iraq, and that most of it goes unreported in the United States. Their argument has some validity, but not a lot. As a *New York Times* reporter commented to the journal *Editor and Publisher* on October 4, 2004: "What good news are we supposed to be reporting when the murder rate in Baghdad has gone up twenty-fold or more since we entered the city last year, and when we can't even walk the streets?" Even as it is, the United States gets a more positive view of the war than the rest of the world—including the United Kingdom, our ally. Most of the world's media outlets differ from us in the picture they present. Why doesn't that picture get into our sitting rooms? Here is part of an email sent around to colleagues in September 2004 by *Wall Street Journal* correspondent Farnaz Fassihi in Iraq. It was a more personal opinion than correspondents generally choose to publish in the paper—perhaps *too* personal—but Fassihi seemed bent on conveying to readers what it was really like:

> Iraqis like to call this mess "the situation." When asked "how are things?" they reply: "the situation is very bad." What they mean by "situation" is this: the Iraqi government doesn't control most Iraqi cities, there are several car bombs going off each day around the country killing and injuring scores of innocent people, the country's roads are becoming impassable and littered by hundreds of landmines and explosive devices aimed to kill American soldiers, there are assassinations, kidnappings and beheadings. The situation, basically, means a raging barbaric guerilla war. In four days, 110 people died and over 300 got injured in Baghdad alone. The numbers are so shocking that the ministry of health— which was attempting an exercise of public transparency by releasing the numbers—has now stopped disclosing them.

Fassihi clearly did not think that, for all our access to multiple sources, Americans were getting a true sense of conditions in occupied Iraq—or perhaps that they didn't want to. (Soon after the email had shot around the world, the reporter was sent out of Iraq on vacation by her employers until after the U.S. election, and a top *Wall Street Journal* official described her situation as "very sensitive"—the fate of most whistleblowers.)

Conversely, for the first time, monolithic Arab states are being exposed via satellite and Internet to a wide array of outside media input. And evidently these new media streams have, apparently, only exacerbated their anti-Americanism. Indeed, the more exposure to other sources of news, the more they seem wedded to their prejudices. The same goes for China and Russia. The freer flow of information, apparently, does not lead all societies toward the same values. Given the freedom to do so, we don't even *perceive* the same things. The truth gets fractured, everybody takes sides, no one knows what's going on, *so people watch the news that confirms their views.*

In our country, the Fox News Channel illustrates this precisely. Uncomfortable facts simply get ignored, or quickly forgotten by their commentators and the people who applaud them. Here's a simple test: How many Bush voters spend much time dwelling on the Abu Ghraib abuses? Few, if any. On the other hand, Al Jazeera is no bastion of impartiality either. No Arab channel will happily tell its viewers that the practice of kidnapping and beheading hostages goes against the Koran, and that numerous Islamic religious figures approve it nonetheless. As the Iranian exile commentator Amir Taheri noted in a September 30, 2004, *Wall Street Journal* Oped, "One of the founders of the Islamic Republic in Iran, Ayatollah Khalkhali, wrote: 'Among those we seize hostage or kill, some may be innocent. In that case, Allah will take them to his paradise. We do our job, He does His.'" No, Al Jazeera will not tell its viewers that their religious leaders are barbaric—for the simple reason that it will lose viewers.

Yes, commercial exigency, rather than the old state-imposed variety, dictates that news channels don't tell viewers what viewers don't want to hear. The reason is simple: Now more than ever—anywhere in the world—viewers can simply switch to another channel, to an alternative view that makes them feel more comfortable. The profit motive can distort the news as surely as state control does. In the brave new world of media, information flows more freely, but certainly not more impartially or accurately. Around the world, more choice has meant more polarization of views, and easier manipulation of news. We, in America, who pride ourselves on our open society—the basis of our triumph over the Soviets—pioneered this system. Yet, like others, we are locked into our delusions. We are no more hearing the world than they us.

So my friend Garrick Utley's observation needs to be updated. Yes, the Soviets' efforts to manipulate and limit their public's access to varied news sources ultimately failed. And the Soviets paid for it. But today's regimes—such as China or the Arab countries, or indeed most halfway-developed countries—manipulate their public more effectively, using lessons they learned from America. Since they can no longer stop it, these nations now allow TV news competition. On one hand, it gives the illusion of variety; on the other, it generates bottom-line fever—which in turn leads to more entertainment, more gossip and scandal, and less real news. In that thin intellectual atmosphere, television news barely has the will or wherewithal to resist spin, to make a complex case for or against anything—and certainly not against strident patriotism or religion. News independence gets especially weak if corporate owners have higher business agendas. Indeed, these days governments deliberately allow corporate owners of news channels to prosper in other businesses.

All over Eastern Europe, oligarchs who own large chunks of national industries also own television channels, and many of these power brokers are cozy with politicians. State, commerce, and news work together to enrich rival elites and to spin the news for each. And ultimately the more conglomerate-owned channels there are, the more uniform the headlines become, as everyone fights for the mainstream advertising dollars. Does any of this sound familiar? Surely I'm not suggesting that this applies to the United States? Well, yes, I am. After all, the owners of Big Media now occupy more and more of the public airwaves, with less and less obligation to serve anything other than their bottom line. The state actively colludes in the process through its regulatory body, the FCC, by constantly giving away public rights to broadcasters almost unconditionally—they don't even pay a fee, as they do in, say, the United Kingdom. All of which puts the state firmly in bed with Big Media, and means that profit wins over hard news.

Does the state, therefore, control American news in any way? It's a hard one to answer. The best answer is that it doesn't need to, for all the reasons we've seen in previous chapters: fewer news resources, groupthink, powerful spin. The news doesn't much get in the way, these days, if the White House spin machine is firing on all cylinders. The unquestioned rush to war in Iraq proves that.

Does that mean there's no open hashing out of issues in the United States? What about the vigorous, divisive crossfire between Democrats and Republicans, between political candidates, or between both sides' media apologists? Yes, certainly, there's no gainsaying the existence of loud open public debates in America. And they exist too in France, Germany, Sweden, the United Kingdom, the Ukraine, Turkey, Poland, even in Serbia and Lebanon. But all those debates are contained within a cultural framework too. We look at them and see their limits or biases. They look at us and see our limits. *But much of the time we don't see beyond our own limits.* That is, we often don't get all the news that's relevant, even very important parts of it. Other countries see things we don't, through the different focus of their news media. And they would say they know more.

What do they know that we don't? One way to determine that is to review the news as it's reported in the United States with the way it's reported in other countries. Whether our version or theirs is closer to the mark depends, of course, on your viewpoint. But the degree of our ignorance and bias matters more because we are the lone superpower, which reserves to itself the right to change the order of things in the rest of the world. Today, as we flex those muscles, our soldiers are at risk, and ultimately our homeland, too. We need to know more; we need to be better than other countries in smoking out the truth.

As the 2004 presidential election loomed, the political battle raged stateside over whether things in Iraq were improving or worsening. Astonishing: Only in the United States could the debate even have existed—not because the American press is freer, but because everyone else, even many Americans in Iraq, could see how bad things were. As one *Boston Globe* reporter in Iraq put it, "To write about the repainting of a school when three car bombs go off killing how many dozens would be irresponsible journalism." Sure, we could have enough faith in the rosy White House version—that we continue to fight and win in the long run with great hardship and bloodshed. And of course we must hope that we do win. But that doesn't mean we weren't deluded in the first place by believing that version.

With the cooperation of former Bush White House Treasury Secretary Paul O'Neill, Ron Suskind wrote the highly critical book *The Price of Loyalty.* Suskind then wrote a celebrated article in the October 17 issue of the *New York Times Magazine* titled "Without a Doubt," in which he reports conversing with an aide to the president:

> The aide said that guys like me were "in what we call the reality-based community," which he defined as "people who believe that solutions emerge from your judicious study of discernible reality." I nodded and murmured something about enlightenment principles and empiricism. He cut me off. "That's not the way the world really works anymore," he continued. "We're an empire now, and when we act, we create our own reality. And while you're studying that reality—judiciously, as you will—we'll act again, creating other new realities, which you can study too, and that's how things will sort out. We're history's actors . . . and you, all of you, will be left to just study what we do."

A chilling passage—and the perfect embodiment of the "not listening" doctrine and its rationale. All presidents to some degree shape the prevailing political mood of their era. President Clinton's lack of interest in foreign affairs fostered national self-centeredness, and the news media's ostrich-like resistance to foreign topics. The George W. Bush era, amazingly, has managed to take Clinton's lead one step further, by actively rejecting outside voices or invocations of outer reality (as in Iraq) as somehow partisan or weak or passive. In other words, in the Bush world, everybody projects forth an insular dream and the most powerful actors simply make theirs come true by force. Nothing is real or delusional. There is no reality in Iraq, only competing visions. Hence Fox News can reflect an Iraq according to one vision and Al Jazeera another, and both can feel equally justified, until one side wins.

And we're back to that old saw: the first casualty of war is truth.

D oes it matter that we don't listen to the world? All this talk of everyone hearing everyone else—is it really no more realistic than a John Kerryesque joining of hands with the UN and bringing harmony to the world through extra sensitivity? After all, the United States was brutally attacked by barbaric murderers: Does it really follow that we just need to listen more? That we should worry more about what the world thinks of us? The answer—if we wish to prevail against the enemy—is yes. As President Bush has emphasized repeatedly, this will be a long struggle, comparable to the Cold War in length, only hotter. A lot of pundits argue, quite correctly, that where the United States has succeeded in fighting off threats to freedom worldwide, it has done so mostly by not listening too much—and through unilateral initiative, often in the face of resistance from allies. Pundits cite the resistance to President Reagan's stand against Libya, the riots against his basing of fresh missiles in the Germany in the early 1980s, President Clinton's unpopular incursions into Serbia and Kosovo, and the like. And they're not wrong: Too much listening to others can cause paralysis. On the other hand, to wage a successful protracted conflict "on many levels" (a phrase oft-used by the White House), you have to know the

enemy's thinking in order to counter it. You have to fight ide-
ologically, diplomatically, financially—you have to fight per-
suasively. In other words, even if you subscribe to the Bush
doctrine of dreams imposed by force, you'd better understand the reality beyond if you want to make others buy into
your dream.

Americans have no idea why Islamism holds any popular
appeal. Unlike the Cold War generation, who had a basic understanding of socialist ideas, Americans have no idea how Islamist thinking might challenge their own around the Muslim
world. How many know who Ibn Tulun, or any other published Islamist ideologue, might be? And what are we doing to
persuade Muslims that our notions of freedom or democracy
or tolerance are good for them? In a region dominated first by
the British Empire, then by dictators, how much can people
identify with the benefits of western-style democracy? We
have not thought enough about who "they" are to know exactly at what level to pitch our ideas. And even if we did, how
to do it? In the post-Soviet 1990s, the United States de-funded
and dismantled much of its "public diplomacy" capability—
in other words, its propaganda machine. The stand-down
happened under President Clinton, but with pressure from a
Newt Gingrich-led Republican Congress. Just as the intelligence services couldn't find enough Arabic speakers to employ
after 9/11, neither could the State Department or the military.
We had let our guard down almost entirely. And the Bush
White House showed virtually no interest in the war of ideas.
In this, as in so much else, the president set the tone. To quote
from a November 2004 London *Spectator* book review by
Jonathan Mirsky: "In August 2002, Mr. Bush said, 'I'm the
Commander—see, I don't need to explain. That's the interest-
ing thing about being President. Maybe somebody needs to

explain to me why they say something, but I don't feel like I owe anybody an explanation.' "

One propaganda disaster followed another: confusion over the *casus belli* in Iraq, the looting of Baghdad museum, Abu Ghraib, no WMD, letting Christian evangelists proselytize in Iraq. Where was the propaganda effort to counter these disasters in the Arab world? As mentioned in Chapter 4, the all-important job of running pro-allied news in Iraq was given, for almost a year, to a California defense contractor called Science Applications International Corp. (SAIC) which had no experience of running newspapers, radio or television. Its efforts became a laughingstock: Iraqis watching this charade wondered about America's competence, about its respect for the local population, and inevitably about its motives. An invasion force with no convincing desire to win over the locals? What could they be after? Oil? And even if it's the oil we're after, surely we should either disguise our motives better, or persuade the locals that they will benefit in the end. As one old Cold Warrior veteran of Radio Liberty told me on condition of anonymity, "We won the Cold War propaganda by persuading the nations under Soviet rule that we cared more about their welfare than the Russians did, indeed that we knew more about their history and culture. We won the Cold War culturally. Today, we're not even fighting a war of ideas—only of bullets."

In an opinion essay he wrote for the *Washington Post* soon after 9/11, Richard Holbrooke said: "Call it public diplomacy, or public affairs, or psychological warfare, or—if you really want to be blunt—propaganda. But whatever it is called, defining what this war is really about in the minds of one billion Muslims in the world will be of decisive and historic importance." He went on to ask (about Osama bin Laden):

"How could a mass murderer who publicly praised the terrorists of September 11 be winning the hearts and minds of anyone? How could a man in a cave out-communicate the world's
leading communications society"? Holbrooke said this even
before the invasion of Iraq. He understood early on that the
American strategy crucially lacked a central pillar, an omission that even Secretary Rumsfeld acknowledged publicly in
an October 24, 2003, interview in the *Washington Times*:
"We are in a war of ideas, as well as a global war on terror.
Ideas are important, and they need to be marshaled, and they
need to be communicated in ways that are persuasive to the
listeners."

In not listening to the world, we are overlooking the importance of countering hostile ideas—even though this failure
affects the security of our soldiers, and ultimately our own national security. The vicious rumor that Jews planned the 9/11
attacks, for example—that no Jews died there because they
were all forewarned—is of course vile nonsense. But much of
the Muslim world doesn't know it to be nonsense—we just assume that they should. In fact, millions of Muslims still believe
that canard. And since they suspect that Washington colludes
with Israel on everything, many of them also believe the
United States itself colluded in 9/11. Why? To create a pretense to launch a crusade against Islam and seize control of its
vast oil reserves. Neither the U.S. government nor the media
have done anything effective to refute the conspiracy theory
among those most likely to believe it. Where are the thorough,
exhaustive documentaries, the point-by-point refutations, the
lists of Jews who died? Why aren't they being beamed into
the Muslim world? Perhaps there's not enough profit in it
for the big news channels. Or perhaps Americans don't care to
soil our hands with such work. On the left, liberal conscience

won't let us acknowledge that other cultures can be so low as to think such things. On the right, we think "they" don't deserve an answer—just bullets and occupation. We are blocking out reality. Listening to others can be a sympathetic activity, but it can also be akin to eavesdropping on the enemy's communications in order to fight better. Either way, we cannot afford not to do it.

As I've said, the United States has a long history of not listening to the world, of being impervious to views and realities in other countries. And on the whole, by sheer wealth and force, we have made our version come true. Perhaps we should be proud of that record, but in truth it's no cause for complacency. Two important reasons: It's an arrogant admission of our ignorance, and it implies that we are willing to go through the hardship and bloodshed that playing catch-up demands of us, usually because we've left it so late that war becomes the only option. Instead of putting the pressure on our soldiers at the eleventh hour, there's a better way. Put pressure on our news chiefs to keep the public better informed. Most Americans have no idea how exactly important foreign news gets excluded. How, practically speaking, does the flow of information from a vast army of official and freelance American reporters from around the world get filtered out? We've seen how, when done deliberately, news can get excluded—through invisible internal clout, hidden spin, or political bias. But much of the time foreign news gets excluded in more mundane but equally crippling ways—for reasons of expense, or disinterest and ignorance. Not listening to what our far-flung stringers and correspondents want to tell us is a central part of not listening to the world. Home office editors and producers assume (and encourage) lack of interest by the public. My experience trying—unsuccessfully—to report the Shah of Iran's impending fall is a typical example.

Americans sometimes wonder why the rest of the world doesn't want to copy us. Can't the Arabs see that democracy has made our country the most powerful in the world? Why can't the French see that Americans are selflessly spending money and lives to bring American values to the people of the Middle East? Can't the rest of the world see the difference between the American way of life and all those failed states in what we used to call the Third World? The answer, of course, is that the rest of the world does not see things as we do because, in many places, their media show them a different world, a world in which America is often the villain rather than the hero. America, in turn, ignores or rejects what others see, and the world is utterly polarized. Here are some examples of what I mean.

KAMA ADO BOMBING: DECEMBER 2001

On December 2, 2001, CNN reported that the U.S. military had officially denied reports "that bombs from overnight U.S. air strikes killed dozens of civilians in two villages in eastern Afghanistan." Major Brad Lowell, a spokesman for the U.S. Central Command, claimed that the planes were attacking a cave and tunnel complex, and there was no proof that errant bombs had destroyed the village of Kama Ado. "It just did not happen," Major Lowell said. "There were no buildings in view to depict or suggest residential areas."

But on December 4, in a front page story in the British *Independent,* reporter Richard Lloyd Parry wrote of the devastation and death that greeted him when he reached Kama Ado. The headline read: "A Village Is Destroyed, and America Says Nothing Happened." Describing the damage and mass graves, Parry wrote: "There has been no retraction of that initial decisive statement: 'It just didn't happen.'" The story, complete with the Pentagon's denial, was picked up by media around the world.

The same day, ABC News featured a story, shot in Qarah Bagh, another Afghan village, that showed villagers standing amidst the rubble of their former homes, telling a translator that they were happy that the Taliban had been bombed.

GERMANY STINKS: MARCH 7, 2003

The American media tried to make light of the political hostility in this country toward France and Germany after their refusal to join President Bush's "coalition of the willing." American viewers heard a lot about things like the move to rename French fries "freedom fries," and the dwindling sales of French cheese and German wines. But European reporting covered the darker side of the story. The popular weekly news magazine *Der Spiegel* exposed the hate-filled language of new "harassment web sites" such as germanystinks.com and francestinks.com, which raised the ugly specters of fascism and betrayal. *Der Spiegel* quoted the rhetoric of germanystinks.com:

> It is the stink of collaboration and cowardice emanating from Berlin and Bonn that we're talking about, where a communist cop-battering gangster foreign minister [Joschka Fischer] and a "win-at-any-price" anti-American popinjay

of a chancellor [Gerhard Schröder] lead the nation that we rebuilt from the ashes of fascism further and further away from our friendship and forgiveness.

UNITED STATES PLAN TO BOMB NORTH KOREA: APRIL 2, 2003

The daily newspaper *The Australian* was the first news outlet to report that, according to "well-informed Canberra sources close to U.S. thinking," the Pentagon had detailed plans to bomb North Korea's nuclear plant at Yongbyon within six months, if the communist state went ahead with reprocessing of spent nuclear fuel rods that would yield it enough plutonium for half a dozen nuclear weapons.

It wasn't the first hint of such a plan ever reported by the press. In 1999, CNN had reported that five years earlier the United States had entertained thoughts of such a bombing upon first hearing of North Korea's plans to develop nuclear weapons. But there was no official comment in 2003, after the Australian story was picked up by news outlets in China, South Korea, Pakistan, and around the world.

ABUSE OF CHILDREN AT ABU GHRAIB: JULY 5, 2004

A German TV newsmagazine called *Report Mainz* broadcast an eight-minute segment reporting that the International Red Cross had found at least 107 children in coalition-administered detention centers in Iraq. Their shocking footage showed armed U.S. soldiers bursting into a home and terrorizing a family with three little children. They also quoted a June 2004

UNICEF report that stated that children were routinely arrested and "interned" in a camp in Um-Qasr.

The story spread quickly. It was picked up by Australian ABC Radio, and by TV2 and NRK television in Norway. The Norwegians reacted so intensely to the allegations of child abuse that the Norwegian press speculated that they might even lead to a change in Norway's participation in the U.S.-led coalition. Al Jazeera said they had two reporters unjustly imprisoned at Ab Ghraib who had witnessed the child prisoners. The Pentagon admitted that around sixty teenagers, "primarily aged 16 and 17," were being detained, but the story has not yet been fully investigated by the American media.

ITALIANS FALL OUT OF LOVE WITH SIMONAS: OCTOBER 2, 2004

At last, good news amid the grim beheadings of hostages in Iraq. On ABC News on October 2, 2004, Peter Jennings announced the release of Simona Pari and Simona Torretti, two Italian aid workers, kidnapped on September 7 and widely reported to have been beheaded. When they returned home, Italy's press received them as heroines. Most of America's press celebrated, too.

But there was virtually no follow up in the United States when the public mood in Italy turned against the two women. In a press conference soon after their return, the "two Simonas," as they were dubbed, gave their backing to the Iraqi insurgents opposing the allied forces. "If you ask me about terrorism, I'll tell you that there is terrorism and there is resistance. The resistance struggle of people against an occupying force is guaranteed by international law," Simona Torretti said.

The Turin newspaper *La Stampa* reported that the national unity in celebration of their return had been short-lived, ending soon after they arrived wearing kaftans and thanking their captors in Arabic on Al Jazeera for their release. They also thanked Italy's Islamic community for working for their release before thanking the government and the Italian Red Cross. Some papers claimed that the government had agreed to pay a $1 million ransom for their release, and this caused bitter divisions in Italian society. The women also called for Italian peacekeeping forces to be brought home, and announced thy planned to return to Iraq. None of this aftermath was broadcast on the network news.

U.S. USE OF DEPLETED URANIUM: 2003–2004

The accusations had been appearing in the foreign press for years: that American deployment of depleted uranium during the first Gulf War had led to the mysterious illness known as Gulf War Syndrome—and that it was being used again in the current Iraq conflict. On March 18, 2003, the BBC reported that moves to ban depleted uranium ammunition in Iraq were considered by the U.S. Department of Defense to be "just an attempt by America's enemies to blunt its military might." Colonel James Naughton of U.S. Army Materiel Command said that Iraqi complaints about depleted uranium (DU) shells had "no medical basis." According to a report in the British newspaper *The Guardian* on April 25, an estimated one to two thousand tons of DU had been dropped on Iraq since the start of the Iraq war—roughly three to six times the amount dropped in the 1991 Gulf War. On September 7, 2004, Al Jazeera claimed that the use of these "weapons of mass destruction" had caused Iraqis in the southeast of the country to have record levels of cancer and babies born with horrific birth defects.

These are just random samples of the way the media in other countries see America and the world: just drip after drip in the steady stream of nasty little facts that help shape other peoples' opinions of America. The point is that there is no world television, no world newspaper; each country sees things through its own filter. What we see as news, they see as propaganda, and vice versa.

I am certainly not suggesting that American news media are more biased or deluded or ignorant than Al Jazeera or French broadcasting—though *they* certainly would. But I do contend that we are as locked within our limitations as the best of them—for the same reasons. The comforting old black-and-white model of Soviet fiction versus American truth doesn't hold up anymore. Most countries have followed the American media model to some degree; satellite technology and Internet access have enabled, and forced, them to. In the Middle East and elsewhere, most people can get the world's many satellite broadcasts, see what everyone else thinks, and access more of each other's views. As exiled Iranian intellectual Amir Taheri comments in a November 1 *Wall Street Journal* editorial: "This modern Arab-Islamic world is 'wired' in the extreme. With startling velocity, it moved from the age of the transistor radio, to that of the cassette, then the satellite channels, and the Web sites."

Yet the paradoxical outcome of all this is that we're not hearing each other. All this free expression hasn't opened many minds. We do keep hearing that the Internet has transformed the world. Throughout the late 1990s Internet boom,

Thomas L. Friedman, the *New York Times* columnist, told us repeatedly that all totalitarian states were about to disappear, overwhelmed by too much truth from outside. In a September 24, 2004, opinion column in the *Wall Street Journal,* Daniel Henninger predicts that the old Big Media control of "content and context" in the United States is about to disappear due to the rise of Internet blogs. So Garrick Utley's forecast still has many adherents. The reality? In fact, increasingly, we all tend voluntarily to shut out each other's truths, both at home and abroad. Likewise, in many countries governments still exercise state control over their media to one degree or another, without repercussions from their public. The Russians and Chinese openly control their many channels, but the phenomenon isn't limited to communist (or former communist) states: after all, Italy's Prime Minister Berlusconi simply owns much of Italian television.[2] Most Arab countries have state-controlled media, and the competition from satellite channels such as Al Jazeera, Al Arabiya, and the U.S.-funded Al Hura, has not changed that. Indeed, if anything, the proliferation of channels has taken the pressure off state-controlled channels to make any internal change. And America's claim to the banner of free speech is not entirely pure: the United States openly closed down the Al Jazeera office in Iraq for being too negative.

These days virtually every country is fighting global terrorism—and everyone has excuses for believing their own prejudices and their own version of reality. The Russians have their own code for reporting on Chechen rebels, who are all depicted as terrorists and seen as part of the common enemy of the West in the war on terror. In their account, the fight against terror quickly becomes the fight to restore empire, and loyalty to Russia becomes an argument for censorship. When an issue is framed in terms of patriotism vs. terrorism, it's amazing how many people will vote willingly for the censoring side—as we saw in the recent Ukrainian elections, when virtually half the country sided with the Russians in attempts to silence the other half.

In many such crisis points, some journalists do emerge to attempt to break the censorship.[3] We owe a special word of thanks to the courageous journalists of Ukrainian television, who broke the rules and decided to report on both sides of their fraudulent presidential election. At 7.30 P.M., on November 26, 2004, just before the evening news was scheduled to begin, the management and news team of Channel 1+1 in Kiev, the leading private Ukrainian channel, stood in front of the cameras while one of them read a statement: "We take full responsibility for the distorted information aired on our channel under the direction of various political forces. From now on we will give only objective and truthful information, and the opinions of all the political parties in the country." But my special hero is the sign linguist who single-handedly struck a blow for freedom when she interpreted the evening news for the deaf the previous night. While the blatantly pro-government script was being broadcast, she explained in sign language, "Don't believe this. It's all lies. Yuschenko [the challenger who lost the first round to vote rigging] is our president and this is probably my last day at work."

On the other hand, Fox News Channel has its own way of ensuring its employees toe the company's conservative line. Daily editorial memos to the staff from the network's senior vice president for news, John Moody, laid down do's and don'ts for the staff. A memo on March 23, 2004, decreed that the 9/11 commission hearings were "not 'what did he know and when did he know it' stuff. Do not turn this into Watergate." On April 6, 2004, he warned, "Do not fall into the easy trap of mourning the loss of US lives and asking out loud why we are there?" When the memos were leaked to the public, Moody rejected "the implication that I'm controlling the news coverage."

And the facile argument that truth will triumph if the system allows maximum free enterprise? In today's megalithic corporate environment, with news channels freely brought and sold by conglomerates, that doesn't hold anymore either. As we've already seen, the system of self-monitoring media, as pioneered after the Cold War in the United States, has massive flaws. The forces of spin distort the already thin news content in ways both invisible and undeniable. It's a prospect the Romans might have recognized: The populace is distracted by spectacle on television while commercial pressures hobble the news. As Ralph Nader never tires of telling us, the free market would be fine if it were truly free. Instead, corporate influences effectively curb the market in a thousand ways, whether through quiet deals inside Washington or by arrangements the conglomerates make with other governments. Who criticizes Rupert Murdoch for going easy on China in return for satellite broadcast deals there? Who knows how investment abroad by channel-owning corporations affects news reports of outsourcing? And how does that affect Washington's attitudes to the flight of jobs abroad?

And our media emulators abroad have learned our tricks. In France, the leading conservative daily, *Le Figaro,* has been taken over by Serge Dassault, the dominant French arms manufacturer. Another conglomerate, Lagardere, which makes missiles as well, presides over a large number of popular French periodicals. Together, Dassault and Lagardere own more than 70 percent of the French press. In August 2004, Dassault met with the journalists at *Le Figaro.* According to a transcript of the meeting made by participants, he told them: "There are times when it's necessary to take many precautions. There are articles that talk about contracts under negotiation. There is some information that is more bad than good. And this puts at risk the commercial and industrial interests of our country."

Naturally, Dassault has strong ties to the French state. In France, too, pro-French patriotic bias in news coincides with good business, and bonds the sly coziness between the state and news-owning corporations. Their media have their own dubious commercial reasons for news bias. The untrammeled market influence over news channels, the ownership by corporations with profit-making agendas, and the hidden forces of spin coincide there as everywhere else.

For a complex set of reasons, in the brave new "free" market world of multiple news outlets, every country creates its own framework of biases. The system of massive choice sounds ideal, of course, until you look more closely. How can we be expected to decide or know which outlet is reflecting the truth behind a given story or issue, if all we can do is accept the word of one source over another? The inevitable outcome is that people fall back on their previously established prejudices. They favor, and follow, their biases. We cannot dismiss others' biases in other countries by pointing to our superior system—because our system now exists everywhere to a greater or lesser degree, and even in America it operates pretty imperfectly. When a system of infinite choice leads only to choosing one's preconceived biases, the system has certainly failed.

Nowhere is this more true than at Al Jazeera, which styles itself a Middle Eastern embodiment of our system. Al Jazeera naturally exhibits all the flaws of the system, and then some. Coziness with the state? Hidden spin? Playing to patriotic and religious sentiment? Guilty on all counts—but it gets much worse. In 2004, when reports began emerging in the Arab press of foreigners who had been bribed by Saddam Hussein with so-called "oil coupons," among the names were several prominent Middle Eastern journalists—including at least one network director.

As massive media proliferation redefines the very meaning of "news," our times have begun to recall the pamphlet-based journalism of our founding fathers' day—or, at their worst, a darker age of confusion and superstition. Remember that, in the first decades of the Republic, newspapers acted as mouthpieces of political factions. They printed all manner of scurrilous *ad hominem* attacks on the great national figures of the time we revere today. In those early days, American publications were even more regional than today—even after the railroads came in—and they tended to reflect the power of regional moguls. The state of affairs endured well into the 1930s: Hearst newspapers printed whatever their owner, William Randolph Hearst, wanted, and everyone knew it. The notion of "objective" or impartial news, rather than opinion or commentary, was centuries in the making; though we take it for granted today, it became an expected standard only after World War II.

How did that standard emerge in the first place? I suspect the process echoed the evolution of the London *Times,* in which the sense of authority and wider responsibility grew with Britain's increased global commitments throughout the nineteenth and into the twentieth centuries. With the world—and history—looking on, news conveyors felt they had to serve higher standards than merely the pleasures or prejudices of consumers. In today's Britain, Rupert Murdoch-style tabloidism has swept away much of that in the United Kingdom—with the BBC still holding out (despite the Gilligan debacle)—and is damaging it in the United States. According to an inside source at Murdoch's *New York Post,* for example, when faced with the final authoritative October 2004 report on the absence of WMD in Iraq, the paper simply didn't address the matter, because it found no way to spin it in favor of the White House. The report, which was on front pages everywhere, simply didn't exist as news for the *Post.*

Many argue that Murdoch and his like are entitled to whatever approach they like, so long as everyone else doesn't follow their example mulishly. That argument may have sufficed in pre-9/11 days. But tabloidism—and the insularity, deafness to foreign affairs, immersion in local crime and celebrity, and know-nothing jingoism that come with it—are a palpably self-destructive force in a country at war. In the ideal Murdoch world, the country would be staring in a mirror applauding itself and laughing at stereotypes of barbarians beyond. Yet all the while, of course, our real enemies would be massing outside—and what enemies, with what motives or ideas or strategies, we would have no way of knowing. Such a world offers the seductive appeal of late Roman decadence: bread and circuses for the people, fake triumphant processions for the leaders, and continuous declarations of bogus victories abroad. That way, ultimately, lies a kind of new dark age. As we carry on in our willful blindness, blocking out those awkward, uncommercial realities in favor of the comforts of prejudice, we risk descending, to borrow the words of the poet Matthew Arnold, into a world "swept with confused alarms of struggle and flight/Where ignorant armies clash by night."

CHAPTER SIX

VOICES INSIDE
THE INDUSTRY

Journalists can be as reticent as doctors or bankers when it comes to airing their dirty linen in public. We are in the business of criticizing everybody else, but when it comes to talking about our shortcomings, we keep it to ourselves. Nevertheless, the steady drumbeat of public criticism of the news media—and the realization that most people seem to have a low opinion of journalists these days—has begun to get under our collective skin. We worry about what's going wrong in the news business and we talk about it constantly, mostly in private. Andy Rooney, the veteran CBS News commentator (and World War II correspondent) recently remarked to me: "You go out to lunch with a bunch of guys in the news business and they talk about what you are talking about—the ethics of the business. I don't think people in the insurance business go out to lunch and talk about the ethics of the insurance business."

With that in mind, I interviewed the three anchors of the big broadcast networks—two of whom were about to turn over the reins to younger men—and some past and present news executives who have reached the top levels of our profession, as well as some of my colleagues in the field. I wanted to know whether they shared my concerns. Did they agree that we have failed in our public duties? How candid would they be about it? After all, Tom Brokaw, who anchored the *NBC Nightly News* for twenty-one years; Dan Rather, who held the longevity record with twenty-four years at the helm of the *CBS Evening News;* and Peter Jennings, who at age 66 is not yet ready to bow out at ABC's *World News Tonight,* have presided over the decline of the evening news as a national institution. If they are genuinely concerned about the state of the news, as they insist when they give speeches to media organizations—and if they are pushing for change, as they claim—why aren't things better? Do they believe that the public has no interest in what happens in the rest of the world? Why does the public think the mainstream media are biased? Not surprisingly, I found the anchors reluctant to criticize their own companies. After all, their employers have made them rich and famous.

As for lower ranking newsmen and women—the working press, who have careers to worry about—they preferred to speak off the record. One promising young CBS News correspondent told me about being asked at three o'clock in the afternoon to do an "in-depth" investigative report for the 6:30 news that evening. The public never knew that the reporting behind that story was paper thin, but the correspondent did. Another colleague, a foreign correspondent stationed temporarily in Israel for another network, told me that his evening news had not done one comprehensive piece on the Israeli incursion into Gaza after weeks of brutal bombardments that killed more than one hundred Palestinians. Working newspeople face these frustrations constantly. They realize they are forced to cut corners, they know that they have important news and insights to report which they can't get past the gatekeepers, and they usually have no choice other than to hold their tongues or quit. But the people at the top must surely have a duty to speak out, and so I interviewed them—on the record.

Andy Rooney, who has a reputation for saying what he thinks both on the air and off, was by far the most outspoken interviewee. Rooney is not an anchor, of course, but as a staple of the *60 Minutes* team, he is an observer who's experienced the news business at close range for decades. One of the first subjects he raised when I went to see him in his cluttered *60 Minutes* office was his colleague Dan Rather. At the time, we were speaking, CBS News was awaiting the report of the two-man independent commission formed to probe the questionable memos that Rather had used in the *60 Minutes* report on President Bush's service in the Air National Guard. Rooney pulled no punches.

"This thing that Dan has done is fascinating to everybody in our business," he told me. "I mean, they are all talking about it. And deploring it even while defending him. You know, they're acting as if he's only done this one bad thing—which I don't totally agree with. I think Dan has been—I don't know why; he may not be as smart as they think—but he has been so blatantly one-sided."

That one-sidedness, Rooney acknowledged, amounted to an anti-Bush bias. "I know it" about Rather, he said, "but I shouldn't know that. You shouldn't know that. Twenty years ago somebody was interviewing [Walter Cronkite]. There was a movement to get Walter to run for president. He said, 'They don't know what they are talking about.' He said, 'Wait till they find out I would take every gun away from every American who owned one. See if you want me for president.' "

When I asked Rooney what he thought of charges of media bias, he said: "There is no question. People ask me if I think the media is liberal, and I say but of course I think it is." When the subject of our colleague Bernie Goldberg's recent book *Bias,* which promoted this charge to great effect (and a nice run on the bestseller lists), came up, Rooney admitted that "I got into trouble around here saying he put his finger on something. He did, absolutely."

Rooney returned to the subject of Rather, which seemed to be very much on his mind. "You have got to put your political opinions and interests out of what you are doing. The thing that Dan does—he uses little words that are absolute clues, giveaways to his political opinions. Like saying 'Bush,' instead of 'President Bush' or 'Mr. Bush.' I don't know how many people hear that. A couple of years ago I heard him refer to 'Bush's cronies.' Well, Jesus, 'cronies'—oh, dear! And he does that consistently. Maybe it's stopped now, but a couple of times a week he would do things that were just so obviously slanted and indicative of his political position. Nobody ever pulled him up on that. I don't know why not. You would think someone would tell him it's not the right thing to do."

The big three anchors, as you might expect, were more circumspect. None of them talked about Dan Rather's problems with the National Guard story, which were still ongoing as we spoke, and I made a point of not asking Dan about his case because it was under review. Instead we talked about broader issues—including how well the *CBS Evening News* did its job of keeping the public informed, especially in international news. I asked him whether CBS News had committed too few resources to coverage of the terrorist threat in the years leading up to 9/11. Did we drop the ball? Rather chose his words carefully.

"With hindsight, yes," Rather reflected. "But at the time, I would say we talked about the terrorist threat, the rising—if not tide—the certain rise in radical, violent Islamic fundamentalism." He pointed to a specific example: The network's deliberations over whether to post a permanent correspondent in Egypt in the mid-1990s. "I remember conversations in the period of 1995–97. Anybody who has been there knows [about] the proverbial volcanic country that is Egypt—even the Egyptian government is part of it. We talked about should we post somebody in Cairo, or should we put somebody there on a three-month basis? It was my view and [that of] some others that we should do that. [But] we didn't do it."

Why not? "Money was certainly a factor," Rather says. "These days money is always a factor, nobody can deny that." But not always. "Sometimes it's a difference in editorial judgment. . . . The opposing view was, yes, that story's there—but, one, it's a hard story to get at . . . and, two, it lies dormant for a very long time. The counterargument to that is, well, part of the reason it's dormant is because we aren't there." In Rather's recollection, the idea eventually drifted away in a sea of alternatives: "It was, well, rather than put somebody in Cairo, should we have somebody posted on the Palestinian side of the Israeli-Palestinian conflict? Open a bureau, if you will, or a sub-bureau on that side. It was all discussed at the same time." But nothing ever happened.

When I asked the same question of ABC's Peter Jennings, he did not point a finger at management. Instead, Jennings, who has years of experience in the Arab world, implied that the failings of ABC News in the run up to 9/11 were part of a wider American failing to understand the Middle East:

"Oh, I think our terrorism coverage was not good at all. Which is not to say that we didn't have some people in our shop, including John Miller, who did manage to go and see Osama bin Laden. I would judge us now, in retrospect, against the Hart-Rudman Report. Based on the amount of attention we failed to give the Hart-Rudman Report, we did a pretty lousy job."

I asked Jennings why most of the media had ignored the report of the Hart-Rudman commission, which had accurately warned in January 2001 that terrorists were likely to launch a catastrophic attack on U.S. soil.[1]

"I don't know, to be honest. Except that I think that we, probably like the vast majority of Americans, even in the wake of the Oklahoma [bombing], and 1993 at the World Trade Center, thought that America was probably immune to this kind of thing. I think it's a cultural *naiveté*—which, by the way, we no longer have." Jennings wondered aloud about whether, "in our fascination and passion now in protecting the homeland," the media have failed to provide an alternative to the Bush administration's posture toward the Arab world. He admitted that he had a special interest in the area: "I['ll] declare my bias here a little; we all have biases, but we should declare them. I am on the board of the American University in Beirut. And I have always believed, always believed, that it was one of the most valuable institutions that this country has ever had in the Middle East. So when I see the State Department come along and hire people out of advertising to improve the American image in the Middle East, I get really angry.[2] Because I have lived in the region; I know that not everybody is anti-American. There is less anti-Americanism in the Arab world, I think, that than there is in Europe."

Tom Bettag is executive producer of the ABC News program Nightline with Ted Koppel, which has long been the industry gold standard for hard news reporting with context.

When I asked him to judge how well the media did its job in the decade leading up to 9/11, I expected a straightforward answer—and I got one.

"I think that in terms of reporting the terrorist story, it broke down completely," Bettag told me. "And I think it [was] largely because of the prejudice against foreign news—believing that the growth of Islamic fundamentalism and anti-Americanism was basically a foreign story that wasn't going to come to much, and that we could ignore easily enough."

Bettag agrees that other historic developments distracted us from the growing threat in the Arab world. "There was a convergence of critical things happening," he recalls. "When the Berlin Wall came down, everybody said it's time for the United States to tend to its own domestic problems, that now the Cold War is over and we have some real intrinsic, bad, internal problems that now we have to pay attention to—education, drugs, equal opportunity."

At roughly the same time, Bettag remembers, the networks were undergoing what he calls "the 'three blind mice' takeover . . . by people who were only interested in making money.[3] That was a great cover for saying, *People are not interested in foreign news—and we can cover a domestic story for half the price that it costs to cover a foreign story.* And so the accountants used that argument to push the [idea] that what people care about is domestic news." Suddenly, he says, "almost any kind of a terrorist story becomes quasi-investigative. It's not an easy story to do and it's an expensive story to do, and it was always pushed aside for something that was cheaper. We dropped the ball on the growth of anti-American terrorism. The U.S.S. *Cole* wasn't [treated as] a particularly big story. If you go back and look, what should have been a really important story was the attack on the tourists in Egypt in the Valley of the Kings [on November 17, 1997]. That was a two-day story. It just went away. We at *Nightline* went back a month later, because, we said, nobody really paid attention to it, and we did a week on it." To Bettag and the *Nightline* team, it seemed like "a spectacular story that anybody [could] get interested in. It was Americans and death and destruction. There was no reason to not do it, but we were shocked at how little attention that got. Again, if you go back to the precursors of 9/11, they just didn't get much coverage."

But when I asked Bettag about the absence of critical media coverage of the Bush administration's decision to attack Iraq, he said the fault lay with the administration.

"I think going into Iraq, there was a lot of coverage," he says. "It turns out to have been bad coverage, because—and it's a difficult problem—because of the weapons of mass destruction stuff. It's not that we weren't questioning. The weapons of mass destruction story came out of the intelligence community, where people were saying, *Look, we can't tell you why, but we can tell you our intelligence is impeccable.* And that set aside the question of whether the weapons of mass destruction even existed."

Bettag maintains that the administration's trust-us position on WMD was an act of stonewalling that was virtually impossible to counter. "That made it game-set-and-match: *We must go in and do something, and we will figure out what we do after that.* And that's what kept it from becoming a discussion about our exit strategy, because we believed there was this clear, imminent danger." Even today, Bettag seems defensive about the networks' failure to dig deeper: "I am not sure that we were asleep, and I think going in, there was pretty thorough discussion and we didn't go in willy-nilly. To a large extent we were lied to or the intelligence services broke down—one or the other."

Almost everyone I spoke to inside our business believed the networks are doing an inadequate job reporting world news. Sandy Socolow, whose three decades at CBS News included stints as vice president, deputy director of news, and executive producer for the *Evening News* with both Walter Cronkite and Dan Rather, predicted a bleak future for his organization's foreign coverage: "The CBS London Bureau is not a news bureau. It is a production bureau. It sucks in material and lays it down. They could do the same thing in New York. Essentially, that is what is eventually going to happen."

Peter Jennings defended the performance of ABC News in reporting on events overseas, but conceded the gaps in its coverage: "I think on our broadcast we are doing quite a good job on Iraq and only an occasional job on Afghanistan. I think we are doing a fair job—I'd give us a six or seven—on Islam in general, because I think we could do a piece a day or at least a piece a week in trying to understand Islam to a greater extent. I think we are doing about a six on terrorism generally. I think we are doing badly by not doing more on China."

Indeed, the breakdown in coverage on Asia was one thing all three network news anchors cited as a concern. On the eve of stepping down from his job as anchor of the *NBC Nightly News*, Tom Brokaw pointed to the conflict between European and American "political culture" as an underreported story, but said that "I am mostly concerned about Asia. I think we are very underrepresented in Asia. We don't get there very often. We have somebody in Hong Kong who is excellent. We do all that big part of the world with one guy. You just look at India and China and what's going on in terms of how they are positioning themselves economically, and occasionally culturally, to take us on in the world. In fact, I don't think anybody is doing that very well."

For Dan Rather, the most important challenge facing CBS News is providing more coverage from China. "In my opinion, China's drive to become first a regional, and then a global, full-service superpower—a combined economic and military superpower—in the early part of the twenty-first century, that's the best running story going."

It may be the best story running, but in the first ten months of 2004, Dan Rather ran exactly four stories from China on the *CBS Evening News*. Correspondent Barry Petersen reported them all and none addressed the subjects of the Chinese military or the economy. The subjects were:

1. A light look at a phony Chinese edition of President Clinton's biography;
2. A story on stem-cell research;
3. A story on pandas;
4. Another story on pandas.

None of the anchors seemed to share my intensity of concern at the lack of foreign news and context on their shows, so I tried another tack. I asked Rather what he thought were the consequences of this news gap. "The consequences are that Americans are not as well informed about international affairs and particularly not well informed about international affairs as it directly affects them," he ventured. "A lot of international coverage can be made to mean something—because it does mean something. But television has great difficulty with depth. This is not an excuse. Television is great at doing some things. Terrific at taking you there—that's one of the things we do best. But we do have some difficulty with depth." Well, I tried.

Peter Jennings seemed equally unconcerned when I asked him if he thought the American public is dangerously underinformed. "No, I don't," he answered. "I don't at all. I think that the American public to a greater degree than anywhere else in the world, has an endless stream of possibilities to understand the rest of the world. If they take them." So much for the newsman's responsibility to educate the public.

Tom Bettag, on the other hand, gave a nuanced and candid answer. "In domestic news there is a lot more available," he said, "and a lot more variety and a lot more going on than there would have been, say, in the late eighties and early nineties. We are better off on domestic news. On foreign news, we are dead in the water. It is scandalous and need not be that way."

I asked Bettag what he thought was missing in our international news coverage.

"I think the important thing is not that we are missing this big story and this big story and this big story. I think what we are missing a sense of reality, that what we get [due to inadequate coverage] is an overall distortion. We don't get a sense of the world as it really is. I don't care what foreign news you put on. It can be a fascinating story from Botswana. But how can [we make] people realize that we Americans are a tiny part of a much larger whole and that everybody isn't alike? That's one of our huge American failings—our sense that all human beings are created equal and alike. We don't realize that Iraqis think differently from the way we think. That they don't necessarily subscribe to the things we consider absolutely obvious. The big failure is not having a sense of people around the world, people seeing things differently, having different things to contribute, people we can learn from, and refuting our own insularity, or myopia. That's a big loss."

As Bettag sees it, that myopia is finally catching up with us. "What is hurting us in a big way is the Islamic world's frustration with us—which is not getting very well reported. The largest thing that we are not reporting is the simply grotesque inequity between societies, between our world and the rest of the world. That either makes people resentful, or leads to [the] flood of immigrants that is changing our own society"—a flood that has included a "damaging brain drain" from the Arab countries. "Those are the big stories. Robert Kaplan did a book about chaos theory around the world, the exploding populations and the increasing urbanization and stripping of resources. He overstated the problem, but [what's important is] understanding these huge growing problems in the world that nobody is addressing." But the process of educating the public must go beyond the occasional piece of cultural-tourist reporting, he warns. "We should begin with not trying to throw those stories singly at people, but trying to open their eyes consistently to the fact that there is a world out there. Instead, we are helping people close their eyes."

And what are the consequences of helping people close their eyes?

"A 9/11 suddenly out of no place," he answered, "where people, in disbelief, say *Why do they hate us? Why in the world would anybody hate us?* Which shouldn't be hard to figure out. We suffer the consequences of our doing things, or corporations doing things, in other countries that are truly grotesque, that we would be ashamed [of] if we knew, from labor and human rights abuses to abuse of the land and natural resources. Every now and then something pops up, like blood diamonds, and gets coverage, [that reminds] us that we are doing unpopular things around the world." For the most part, though, Bettag says ruefully, "If it happens overseas, it doesn't happen."

When I asked Andy Rooney how far the American public is from being well informed, he let loose a broadside.

"Oh, a hell of a way. For one thing, they have a great tendency to turn away from the truth anyway. Beginning with religion, for Christ's sake. How are you going to speak truth about anything to a religious community? And America is that religious, largely—eighty percent or more. I can't imagine what news is among the Muslims. Are there any good newspapers there?"

"Not many," I said. "They are mostly government controlled. But there is al Jazeera television."

"We keep attacking it, but it sounds good to me," he joked.

"Do you think there are dangers in being underinformed?"

"Oh, I think so for a democracy," Rooney said. "It is amazing that this democracy has lasted for as long as it has. There is no guarantee that it is going to survive. . . . Look at where the country is going. In the last four years there have been a lot of consequences of a dumb electorate. Letting Bush do the things he has done. The attorney general [John Ashcroft]! I don't think the people are aware of our history in matters of civil rights."

At age 88, Walter Cronkite remains a towering figure in American broadcast journalism. From the CBS Evening News anchor's chair, he helped define the American landscape from 1962 to 1981. Yet after he left the anchor chair, his successor, Dan Rather, could find no room on the Evening News for occasional reports by the man who was widely known as the most trusted figure in American public life. Cronkite still makes numerous appearances and documentaries, but on other networks. In his memento-crammed corner office at the CBS corporate headquarters, I asked him to define the responsibilities of the news media.

"Well, if you are talking about what responsibility management believes we have, and the responsibilities I believe we have, we would be talking at cross points," Cronkite said. "You've got to acknowledge, yes, that they have what they consider responsibilities to shareholders. This has been the story preached by management every time this matter comes up—*they think* it's responsibility to the shareholders. I think the responsibility is to the public, the electorate."

As Cronkite notes, the networks have not yet learned to "balance their two responsibilities. There is no question that they are formed as profit earning institutions, and they have to fulfill that job—unless we want to go for public broadcasting entirely, and then how do you support that? Through appropriation, through government bodies which in turn politically manipulate it. [That] would be worse, probably, than commercial manipulation.

"Meanwhile," Cronkite says, "the networks must understand their responsibility to the populace. It is the responsibility vested in the stations through the Communications Act. The Communications Act provides for a local community to take to the Communications Commission any plea that [a] local station trying to renew its license is not entitled to that license because it is not living up to its obligation to the public. One of the problems we have in the United States," he noted, is that "community groups do not take action against their local stations."

When the subject turned back around to the matter of the media's responsibility to the public, Cronkite's response seemed far more engaged than those of his younger colleagues. "I think that the responsibility is in providing information [about] the community, the nation, the world," he says. "It has frequently been said—and I am inclined to agree—that it is not

the journalist's role to educate. That's up to the education people. It is, however, our role to inform in such a way that the ed-
ucators can have the raw material to teach." Why? Because
without an educated populace the news is a service without an
end user. "We who depend on the intellect at work in the community as our customers for the news, either print or broadcast—we must also be constantly supporting the improvements
in the educational system."

But perhaps Cronkite's most stunning answer came in response to a simple question: "Do you watch the *CBS Evening
News* now?"

"Not regularly, no," said the man who made that very program an American institution. "There's nothing there. There's
nothing there but crime and sob sister material. It's scandal
sheet stuff, tabloid stuff for the most part, I find. That's too
bad. I would like to see it more responsible, if you please."

I also wanted to know whether the anchors shared the current belief in our business that foreign news is bad for sales
and ratings. They agreed that no reliable data seem to support
that belief. Still, they were hard-pressed to explain the dwindling amount of foreign news on network broadcasts in any
other way. Dan Rather put it this way:

"I do not subscribe to the idea that if you lead foreign,
you die—that if you have a broadcast that is fairly heavily in-
fused with foreign coverage, on a day-in-day-out basis, you
lose. I am unconvinced—I started to say totally unconvinced—I am unconvinced that's true." So what explains the
networks' reluctance to feature foreign stories? In Rather's
view, foreign news is simply an easy target for network cost-
cutters. "What happens is, in the evening news broadcasts, so

many things go into deciding whether your ratings go up or down. What comes before you and after you is every bit as important, if not more important, than what's on the broadcast. But when it comes to cost control, when you are looking for things to blame, you get asked, *Why are we [CBS] down two-tenths of a point?* Which, by the way, is a big deal. They say, You know what? That's because you had more foreign stories. Or, did you notice last week that you led three times with foreign news?"

In fact, the *CBS Evening News with Dan Rather* airs roughly one foreign story a night—even including the events in Iraq. Rather told me he has sometimes argued with management over whether to cover a major foreign news story, but he noted that he has had to choose his battles carefully.

"Part of the responsibility in a job such as I have," he said, "is to wage the good fight without fear or favor. And I think we can all be faulted for not fighting hard enough, not taking enough risks to fight. Because who knows if we did, what the results would be?" For years, Rather says, he argued that the *CBS Evening News* needed to be extended to a full hour if it were to do justice to the events of a given day. But in our interview he conceded that he could no longer win an argument with the front office on a question of principle, by talking about the company's responsibility to the public: "It's gone out of fashion. It's gone. To talk in those terms is the equivalent of wearing spats to the office. Or driving a horse and wagon. Basically, you get tagged as yesterday's man, or woman."

Rather was careful to qualify his criticism of the front office. "Don't let me overstate this," he told me. "There is certainly a strain of [idealism] there. When the current war broke out, when the attack was made on Iraq, [Viacom

Co-COO] Les Moonves, who is the decision maker, was prepared to blow out coverage right across the board. And the first night that we did that, we had a terrific night. Nothing to regret. We had smart coverage—a lot of coverage. The audience responded. Now, what happened, unfortunately—a bad break. We were contracted to carry the NCAA basketball tournament, beginning on Thursday night. The war began on Wednesday night." According to Rather, Moonves pushed to preempt the basketball to cover the war live in prime time that Thursday and Friday—"at some cost to himself, and considerable cost to the network." Rather says he gives Moonves credit for trying. "But he got pressure from the people who made the contract: *Hey, the contract—you've got to do it.* And also the affiliates[4] that had a team in the tournament—I won't say all of them, [but] most of them," pressured CBS to go with the basketball. "Les wanted to do what he knew to be in the best interest of public service. He made a lot of telephone calls. There was a lot of maneuvering behind the scenes. But in the end we got *killed,* because the basketball got us off to such a horrible start."

When it comes to deciding how much foreign news to put on the air, the bottom line is clearly . . . well, the bottom line. Dan Rather may be right that cutting foreign coverage is sometimes just the easiest refuge of network bean-counters—but Tom Bettag is also correct when he points out that it costs at least twice as much to cover a foreign story as a domestic story. Andy Rooney sums up the situation with his usual frankness: "Money has taken over news. It was always a factor, but never what it is now. I think it's that these people at the top are driven to make money." His reading of Les Moonves's motives is somewhat different from Rather's: "Moonves, his only desire is to keep the price of the stock up, to make more money for himself," Rooney carps. "And it's the business of winning, too. He wants to win, and his idea of winning is to make more money."

What are the chances that the network bosses are ready to listen to these voices from within the industry? You be the judge. Shortly after Dan Rather announced he was giving up the anchor chair, Les Moonves said he saw an opportunity to pull the *CBS Evening News* out of third place with the near simultaneous departure of Tom Brokaw from *NBC Nightly News:* "It will give us an opportunity to look at what we're doing right and what we're doing wrong and proceed with the future in a different way." The only aspects of the *Evening News* that are not negotiable, Moonves said, are the 6:30 time slot and the half-hour duration.

Journalists constantly insist on greater transparency in the affairs of government and the conduct of public business, and few businesses are more public than broadcast news. Yet when it comes to making public how much their employers pay the nation's leading journalists, an opaque curtain suddenly comes down. Take the question of the amount earned by the evening news anchors of the three big broadcast networks. That's surely a matter of public interest, especially at a time when the networks daily slash news budgets, close foreign bureaus, and prefer cheap news to important news. So I asked Tom Brokaw, Dan Rather, and Peter Jennings how much they make. But first I had a conversation with Don Hewitt, the CBS News executive who invented the evening news format, the presidential debate, and the TV newsmagazine. It was Hewitt himself who raised the issue of salaries, and was remarkably candid on the subject.

"You know, there is a certain hypocrisy on the part of guys like me," he said. "I always point to the fact that Bill Paley put up a wall between news and entertainment, and that wall can never be breached. But once a week I climbed over that wall to get an entertainment-sized paycheck.

"I remember the day—put this in the book—when Walter Cronkite called me into his office, and said, 'Close the door. I just got a phone call from WCCO in Minneapolis. They offered me a hundred thousand dollars a year. Can you believe anybody would pay me a hundred thousand dollars a year?' Most associate producers now make a lot more than that. All of a sudden," he says, "when Barbara Walters got the first million dollars,[5] everybody around here said, *The company's making money like it's going out of style. Where's ours? We are responsible.* We pushed them."

As Hewitt conceded, the salary-mongering got out of hand—jacking up the costs of the network news organizations in the process. "You know, you could go around and play high and mighty journalist, and then leave it to your agent to go make the deal. And he's the same agent who makes the deals for rock stars. Something about that doesn't ring true. We want it both ways. We want to be thought of as separate and above and not part of, but we want to make the kind of money that we are bringing in—well, we are not bringing it in now; the kind of money the company *was* bringing in, from the sweat of my brow." By the mid-1970s, if anyone in CBS management had dared compare Don Hewitt with one of CBS's biggest stars—"You're not Lucille Ball or Jackie Gleason"—Hewitt could respond, "The hell I'm not—I'm making more money for you than they are!" In retrospect, Hewitt sees this dual role as "a schizophrenia that goes with television journalism. We all chose to have the agent, to go into the contract fights, to say to [CBS], *You are not paying me what I'm worth.*" In those days, he says, "I made an obscene amount of money."

And so I asked Hewitt how much he was making at the top of his career.

"Six. *Six!* And I went to them once and I said I would like to give you back a million dollars a year, if you will spread it through the place, if you will give it to the producers, the directors, the kids who work around here. They refused. They did not want to get into that. I am one of the lucky ones. I made enough money to live on the rest of my life. It was a gesture that wasn't going to make any difference to my standard of living—and it might have made a difference to somebody else's."

I told Hewitt that I was slated to talk with Tom Brokaw next. What should I ask him?

"I have already conceded that the guys like me at the top gobbled up so much money that they had to start cutting corners in other places to make sure they kept the money makers, the bread winners, happy. Ask him: Is there a better way to do that? I am sure that Tom makes at least twice the six I made. It may even be close to fifteen now. I don't know. It's just demand. There are two of them, Jennings and Brokaw, in demand. [Tim] Russert is in demand. Russert's good. [Bob] Schieffer's good. I don't think Schieffer makes a tenth of what Russert makes."

A short trip across town to the towers of Rockefeller Center brought me to Tom Brokaw's office—which, by the way, is less than a quarter of the size of Don Hewitt's. I told him the story Hewitt had told me, about how at his height he had offered to give back one million of his six-million-dollar salary if his bosses would spend it on the lesser paid news staff. Brokaw, who was finishing a take-out lunch from a styrofoam container at his desk, thought about that for a moment before replying: "I honestly don't think the economics are that important—what they pay me as opposed to what they spend on news gathering."

So I asked him, "What do they pay you?"

"I am not going to tell you," he said. "I get paid a lot."

"Hewitt thought you are getting paid twelve to fifteen million."

"Yeah. I get paid *a lot.*"

"Does that mean you have fewer bureaus?"

"No, that's not true. You know what, if I got paid less, they'd bank it. They wouldn't spend it. That's the point. That's what you have to understand, Tom. They'd bank it, or they would spend it on other corporate enterprises. Roone [Arledge, former president of ABC News] changed this whole equation by courting Barbara [Walters] and giving her a million dollars a year. And then chasing Dan, and chasing me. You know, he made me a lot of money. He took me into a whole area I never expected to get to, and Roone changed the dynamics of what you pay talent on the air. We were probably underpaid for a long time in what we were earning, and we are probably overpaid now. I don't know what the number is, but they seem to believe by paying me they get a fair return on their investment. And that's the way business operates. But if they paid me a third or a half, they wouldn't take that other half and say, Oh, we are going to spend that money on covering the madrassas of Pakistan, or whatever."

I questioned Dan Rather next on the subject of salaries. We met in the not-very-elegant CBS News building on West 57th Street, in his crowded office one floor above the news room and the anchor set. The décor was very masculine, very Dan. As always, Dan behaved graciously, but he weighed his words carefully: As we spoke, he was in the midst of the National Guard scandal, which would bring his career as CBS anchor to an end just weeks later.

When I repeated Hewitt's story, Dan jumped at the bait. "When do you say he did that?"

"When he was at the top and he was making six million, whenever that was."

"When was that—recently?"

"I didn't ask him when. It sounded like it was a few years back."

"I don't ever recall . . ." Rather thought a moment before continuing. "Let me say this. I don't think this breaks a confidence, which I don't want to do. If he did that—and I would be wary about that, but who knows?—he was not the first to do that. That offer has been made before. This is all I am going to say about it. The offer was: Rather than cut bureaus and cut staff, if there was a giveback, could the giveback money be earmarked to improve news? And the answer, which I am not going to go into any detail about—the answer, in good spirit, was: That's not the way it works. That's generous, even noble, but it's not the way the system works."

"When did you do that?"

"Uh, I have told you all I am going to tell you."

"You know, I asked Brokaw," I told him. "First of all, I asked him how much he makes, because Hewitt said he thought Brokaw was making twelve, fifteen, something like that."

"I have no idea," Dan replied.

"I don't either. He said, 'I am not going to tell you.' He said, 'It's a *lot* of money—a lot of money.' And then we talked about the matter of giveback offers.'

"I think he's the best paid of the three."

So I popped the question to Rather: "How much do you make?"

"I am not going to tell you. I will sure tell you it's less than the other two. But I will also tell you right behind that, that I have no complaints whatsoever."

Finally, I interviewed Peter Jennings. We spoke in the large living room of his Central Park West apartment, with its splendid view overlooking the best part of New York. Jennings's response to the Hewitt story surprised me:

"I did that one year, too. It's foolish. I mean, if the companies wish to spend—Look, the big corporations have chosen how they are going to spend their money. They have chosen how much money they are going to give to the news division. We could indeed operate more efficiently. Our news divisions are burdened to some extent by their relationships with their unions. If we were a non-union shop there would be more money. That's a decision the companies made a long time ago. I remember one year, not too long ago, saying to my lawyer, 'Look, if they'll put the money into x, let's give it back.' He said, 'That's not the issue. They'll be more than happy to take your million dollars back.' And God knows, I make so much money I could afford to give them a million dollars back, but I am not sure we would hire another correspondent or two more correspondents, or five more correspondents."

So I asked him what I had asked Tom and Dan. "How much do you make?'"

"I would never tell you. Of course."

"They told Dan that's not the way the system works."

"I think in some respects they are right."

"Tom never did offer to give money back, but he said if he did, they would just bank it."

"I think he is also right," Jennings said. "I mean, if you took a million dollars from any one of the anchor people's salaries. . . . Let me just talk a little bit about the salaries, so you will have this in context. When I went overseas as a

foreign correspondent, I had four hundred dollars in the bank.
When I came to the United States in the mid-1960s, I made
less money coming here than I was making in Canada. I never
talk very much about that. I will tell you how much I made as
an anchor when I was just a young boy in knee pants. I made
thirty-nine thousand dollars a year in 1965. And it seems a little disingenuous for people who make as much money as Dan
and Tom and I do—and who live as well as we do, and have as
much privilege as we do—to say we would do it for nothing.
Because if the company came along now and said, we would
like you to do exactly the same job for nothing, I would tell
them to stuff it. Because money has become—as it has to do
with anything in public consumption—it has become a measure of authority and power. And that quite frankly is the way
I think it should be regarded."

Just days before our conversation, Jennings noted, he had
spoken about the news industry's priorities, at a rather august venue—the Radio-Television News Directors Associa-
tion awards banquet on October 4, 2004. He recalled the
speech as "the closest I have come to criticizing my management," though he told me that "you will find it so weak, in
your terms, as to be pathetic." At the dinner, Jennings took
on the subject of world news coverage. "The one public thing
I said was, we are not doing enough reporting of the rest of
the world—and I am losing that battle. Everybody in the audience—all [of whom] have been in the business—understood that I wasn't making any more headway with my
employers than they were likely making with theirs, if they
were interested. And I am not sure everybody is interested. I
think if you had the golden opportunity we had to work overseas—in your case to see a bin Laden coming, in my case to
see a Khomeini coming—then we are a little more sensitive

to the fact that where there is smoke there should be a reporter, not merely where there are flames."

Jennings recognized the implication of his argument—that even his highly paid position isn't necessarily all that influential when it comes to deciding what becomes news. "The one legitimate thing to ask the anchor people, it seems to me, is how much power do we really have—and how much power do we exercise? I can't speak for the others, but it seems to me that if you have one of these jobs for which we are paid a ton of money, it's not good enough just to complain publicly" about corporate business decisions. "I have never thought there was anything to be gained by making a public address à la Ed Murrow about the state of the business if it weren't your last resort. And even then, as a last resort, I question—whether it was Murrow or Severeid or Koppel or anybody else—whether or not it has had any effect. The people we should be speaking to are our bosses."

After talking to the three anchors about how much they earn, I talked to a man who has played a key role in pumping up salaries in our industry. Richard Leibner negotiated Dan Rather's handsome contracts and those of a number of other television correspondents—myself included. A figure right out of central casting, Liebner plays the role of agent with zest: He is flamboyant, emotional, and talkative (except when it comes to his clients' salaries). On the day we spoke, however, I found him uncharacteristically downbeat about the future of our business, the networks' drive for ratings and profits, and the dumbing down of the news.

"An argument could be made that the old approach was elitist in its way," Leibner told me. "And an argument could be made that this new approach, driven as it is by focus groups and market testing, is more democratic." But even from his agent's perspective he recognizes that a purely corporate, market-driven news industry is constantly at risk of falling into a dangerous vicious cycle. "The less people know about the things they need to know, the less they will make informed choices when it comes to what they want to know. Before 9/11, for example, how many people would have said that they wanted to know more about places like Afghanistan or Iraq? And you find yourself asking whether we would have approached things differently in either or both of those countries if the American public had known more about them." And this line of reasoning, he concludes, extends beyond the news business to the world at large, "up and down the realm of public affairs, from budgets and deficits, to Social Security and Medicare, to the most basic knowledge about what our Constitution says and how our government works."

A postscript, just to put the discussion about salaries into perspective: In the years he spent running *60 Minutes,* Don Hewitt says, the magazine made more than *two billion dollars* for CBS. As the late, great Fred Friendly said, "When they say it isn't about the money, it's about the money."

CHAPTER SEVEN

HISTORY AND GEOGRAPHY

What We Don't Know Can Kill Us

How many Americans know where Djibouti is, and why it occupies a strategic spot geographically? Why is Chechnya so important to the Russians and why, historically, do Chechens hate the Russians? Why did Greece and Russia help Serbia during the Bosnian/Balkan wars in the 1990s?1 When it comes to world history, politics, and even geography, our educational system is so abysmal that Americans know little if anything about them by the time they start reading the news as adults. And, in general, especially on television, the news does virtually nothing to improve matters. American newscasters will simply tell you, "we don't do history." News spots last no longer than a minute or two; there isn't enough time before the commercials. Result: we have no idea why the events in Bosnia, Rwanda, Chechnya ever happened—and how we might have prevented them, had we known of their history.

For that matter, what do we even know about America's interests abroad? Do we understand why, in the post-Soviet universe, the United States has opened new bases in far-flung countries from Kirghizstan to Georgia, other than the vague sense that our government is fighting terror? Leave aside, for a moment, that such bases cost you, the taxpayer, dearly and you should know why your money is being spent in such places. The Pentagon currently owns or rents 702 bases in 130 countries around the world, plus a number of other bases that are part of NATO or other multilateral commitments.[2] Consider: Do you know whether the United States is welcome in each country? Whether we are backing the right regimes? Whether we know what we are getting into?

In fact, we know very little of what Washington is doing around the world in our name—and we're certainly not going to learn much about it on the nightly news. Even when a major catastrophe—such as the massacre of schoolchildren by Chechen terrorists in Beslan, Russia—captures news attention, we are not told that the United States has a new military base in nearby Georgia. Why are American forces there if not, at least in part, to stop such things? Perhaps the base has a different purpose—if so, what? The answer must surely be found in the region's geography—a region in which Chechnya, Georgia, Armenia, Azerbaijan, Turkey, and Iran abut each other, a region that's awash in oil, terrorists, and countries striving to kick free of Russian domination. If the news won't give us such context, how can the public be expected to monitor and judge its government's activities and competence? Instead, we're shown images of devastated families, and lulled to complacency with vague talk of attempts to "destabilize the region." Why would the whole region be destabilized? And how would it affect America, if at all? Again, no explanations from the news media.

In fact, events in the Caucasus matter enormously to Americans. Our ignorance of the region's geostrategic importance allows our government to operate freely without input or check from us. But it also allows others to maneuver against our interests, without Americans knowing or pressuring their government to respond. That kind of public ignorance does allow an unintended political spin to endure. It has the effect of keeping alive received, and often false or outdated, assumptions. In the years after the fall of the Soviet Union, for example, virtually no American media would carry stories suggesting that the instability in Russia's periphery was a direct result of Russian meddling. Why? Because received opinion in America held that the Russian army and the Russian state were just too poor to mount an effective foreign policy. Russia was too busy trying to remain democratic and capitalist. In the meantime, in many newly independent ex-Soviet states, internal strife and civil wars broke out apparently spontaneously. Yet, in most cases, the outcome favored Russian power. In fact, in Moldavia, in Georgian Abkhazia, in Uzbekistan, in Tajikistan, in Armenia and Azerbaijan, Russian military might intervened to cause unrest, and then to settle it. No American mass news media at the time reported the events as a concerted Russian policy. Indeed, American media relied mostly on Russia's own Interfax News Agency for reports.

In the Azerbaijan-Armenia conflict of the early 1990s, Russians manned parts of the front line on both sides; they supplied both sides with arms; they ran the intelligence and communications on both sides; and they helped Armenia win the civil war. To most Americans, it seemed like an obscure and irrelevant conflict with the daunting name of Nagorno-Karabagh. Yet Azerbaijan holds rights to massive amounts of oil in the Caspian Sea. A powerful and rich independent Azerbaijan supplying the West with oil could offset the oil leverage of Russia and the Middle Eastern countries. The Israelis understood that so well that they opened a military office in the capital Baku, to try to help the Azerbaijanis. But too many other interests were eager to cripple Azerbaijan from the start—Iran just below, Russia above—and so they both helped the Armenians in the war. Russia and Iran became so friendly over the matter that it soon spilled over into nuclear co-operation. The result? The impending Iranian nuclear threat that dominates headlines today. This kind of media blackout can have consequences beyond just an uninformed public: Congress itself was so deluded as to these events—and the real interests of the United States—that it succumbed to pressure from the Armenian-American lobby and slapped an embargo on Azerbaijan during the 1990s. In the meantime, journalists expert in the region's affairs—such as the Montana native Thomas Goltz, who reported for American newspapers on the massacres of women and children by Armenian guerrillas—faced accusations of propagandizing for oil interests and other smear tactics by the American-Armenian lobby. (Goltz wrote the highly readable and authoritative book *Azerbaijan Diary* about his experiences reporting that conflict.)

As usual, Americans had no idea of the stakes and American interests in the matter, nor of who was manipulating them in what direction. It would be a sorry enough saga if it ended there, but the repercussions affect crucial U.S. strategic interests to this day. At this writing, oil prices have risen to near record heights, and in the long term will only go higher with rising demand from China and India. Most of the countries with large strategic reserves of oil—from Venezuela to the Middle East—tend to be either unstable or intermittently anti-American. Many people beyond America's borders still think of the Iraq war as a grab for long-term oil security. The White House denies it, of course, but frankly there's nothing wrong with the Iraq war being, at least in part, over oil. Where else will the United States get easy unconditional access to oil in the years to come? Russia has a kind of veto over all the oil reserves in its former republics, and has successfully fought to keep it that way. Azerbaijan was the only holdout. It wanted to build a pipeline via Georgia to Turkey, giving Azeri oil direct access to western markets while avoiding the veto of both Russia and Iran. Some oil experts will tell you that if Azerbaijan had come on line earlier, Iraq might not have happened.

Instead, Azerbaijan began to fall apart in the 1990s under a U.S. embargo, isolated by the Russia/Iran axis, and losing the war with Armenia. It was held together by the last-minute intervention of a former Soviet Politburo member named Akbar Aliev, who took over as an "invited" leader at first and succeeded in staving off the Russo-Armenian onslaught. In 1998 he won a quasi-democratic election. He held the country together, promised all things to all parties, and stabilized the internal situation forcibly by eradicating dissent. After a decade in power, he died in 2004, to be replaced by his son— with U.S. backing—in what most observers regarded as a rigged national election in Azerbaijan. Finally, the so-called Baku-Ceyhan pipeline from Azerbaijan to Turkey began to take shape on the ground. The United States had woken up to the importance of saving Azerbaijan, but had to do so by compromising on democracy. Imagine the propaganda weapon this furnished the hardliners in nearby Iran. "What? The U.S. wants to spread democracy by invading Iraq?" they say. "Sure, look at the democracy they imposed on Azerbaijan. Next it'll be Iraq, then Iran."

This is the kind of history Americans never get on their news. In some parts of the world, history plus geography equals destiny. Traditionally, America has offered the reverse ethos: an escape from the inherited negatives of longstanding tribal enmities. The American public in the New World doesn't like to think too much about such places and predicaments. But all too often they are strategic zones that matter to us nationally, and some of our American minorities have tribal stakes in the very places they have fled. They take sides, and their voices influence other Americans. Irish Americans on Northern Ireland, Miami Cubans on Cuba, Californian Armenians on Armenia, Jews on Israel—all have their agendas. Some such groups have long hidden alliances with proxy groups. Israelis, for example, currently favor the Kurdish cause in northern Iraq, as veteran investigative reporter Seymour Hersh revealed in a June 28, 2004, *New Yorker* article. For a while Israelis supported the Chechens, because Russia supported Saddam and Syria and Iran. Now, and ever since the Chechens began accepting help from al Qaeda, no one is taking the Chechen side—not even fellow Muslims. The Arabic press has nothing positive to say about the Chechens, and Arabs declare this explicitly, because Russia supports the Palestinian cause. If Russia supports the Palestinian cause, Russia can kill as many Muslim Chechens as it wants.

Which is a great pity, because of all the suffering Muslim communities in the world—indeed among any communities, Muslim or otherwise—the Chechens have suffered the worst. Indeed, they have survived several attempts at genocide. The first came in the 1860s, when Russia began to subdue the mountainous area and purged perhaps half a million Caucasian Muslims. An estimated half of those died. These days, again, the Chechens are undergoing a full-scale genocide at Russian hands. We don't get any of the news or images of their suffering, but they do exist. Children burned in buses. Men fixed in poured concrete and left to starve to death. Women killed with sharp stakes driven into their vaginas. The scale and sheer depravity of Russian conduct in Chechnya is hard to imagine.

Indeed it exceeds what was done to them during World War II when Stalin forcibly stuffed half the Chechen population into cattle trucks and sent them into the frozen wastes of Central Asia, where they died in hundreds of thousands. Russia is at it again, and as usual getting away with murder—this time because of our shared war on terror. What Americans don't know, of course, is that Russia stoked the jihadist elements there, as it did in its other former Muslim republics, in order to create an excuse for intervention. The Chechens won their first war of independence in the Yeltsin era without any help from fundamentalists. It was a nationalist war pure and simple. But Russian authorities couldn't live with Chechen independence—it blocked Russia's control over Georgia, Armenia, and Azerbaijan. Ultimately, it blocked their veto over oil supplies in the Caucasus and the Caspian Sea. So they restarted the war.

Many people, indeed most Russians, believe that their own government engineered the immediate *casus belli,* a series of explosions in Moscow apartment buildings. A good deal of evidence exists showing that the KGB planned and executed the apparent terrorist bombings of obscure Moscow residential blocks, which they then blamed on Chechen terrorists. The Kremlin was bent on retaking the runaway republic, and they set about creating the necessary national mood. Russian officers even secretly sold their own soldiers to Chechen kidnappers in order to heighten tensions. Russian officials wanted to cause chaos and division in Chechnya, and it appears they succeeded. The late Paul Klebnikov of *Forbes m*agazine, who was assassinated in 2004 outside his Moscow office by unknown assailants, outlined all these sinister shenanigans in great detail in his book *Godfather of the Kremlin: Boris Berezovsky and the Looting of Russia.*[3] Klebnikov quotes Russia's former Security Council chief, General Alexander Lebed, on whether the Russian government had organized the residential terrorist attacks against its own citizens. "I'm convinced of it," says Lebed. (Lebed later died in a mysterious airplane accident.)

As Klebnikov writes, "in Chechnya, the Kremlin had been undermining moderates, supporting the extremists financially and politically, and consequently sowing the seeds of conflict." He adds, "the worst case scenario is that the Berezovsky strategy with the Chechen warlords was a deliberate attempt to fan the flames of war. Why would the Kremlin (acting through Berezovsky) want to support the Islamic fanatics that later ended up shedding so much Russian blood?" Klebinov believes it was an attempt by Yeltsin's Kremlin circle—which included Vladimir Putin—to keep power by stoking a patriotic war. (Putin ultimately forced Berezovsky into exile as part of his drive to concentrate power into presidential hands.) One item of evidence, cited by Klebnikov to illustrate Russian complicity in Chechen terror, is a report in the French newspaper *Le Monde* of "the Russian arms-exporting monopoly providing Shamil Basayev's men with weapons."[4] Shamil Basayev later organized the raid on the Nord Ost theater in Moscow that left 130 hostages dead, and the Beslan school atrocity that killed so many children. Basayev is now the leading Islamic terrorist in Chechnya. It's not surprising that, because we work in tandem with Russia on terrorism, so many in the Muslim world believe that the U.S. government too was complicit in the 9/11 attacks. The American public, naturally, has no awareness of such background history.

We can dismiss outlandish conspiracy theories about America that are harbored by paranoid people abroad—after all, the United States is not Russia—but it would be foolish to dismiss their reasons for harboring them, considering the nations we embrace as allies. But the relevance of Chechnya goes beyond our unpopularity among Muslims, and beyond a potential

Chechen terrorist attack on the United States directly. (On October 13, 2004, the *Washington Times* cited intelligence reports that a group of Chechens had secretly entered the United States via Mexico in August.) The events of Chechnya may become a matter of life and death for the United States, worse even than the al Qaeda threat. Let me repeat that: *Worse than the al Qaeda threat.* How is it possible? Consider that after the Beslan school massacre in Russia's North Ossetia province, President Putin declared that he too had the right, around the world, to preempt terror against Russia. Taking a page from the Bush doctrine, he declared publicly that he would intervene in any country he deemed necessary. The statement was reported widely on American news outlets. What your news experts didn't do is ask the simple question: Where could he mean? In almost every applicable country, the United States already has either troops or a deal with the local government.

The most immediate possibilities would be Georgia and Azerbaijan. The largest communities of recently exiled Chechens, often accused of aiding and abetting terror, live in those nearby countries. Russia keeps a base in Georgia by main force, despite Georgian protests. And it maintains a threat over Azerbaijan via the Armenians. But the United States also has a base in Georgia and massive pipeline investments from top American oil companies in Azerbaijan. If Russia launched raids into either country, it would soon conflict with American interests—and Russia still deploys a formidable arsenal of nuclear weapons pointed at American shores. It may seem unlikely, but by this logic Putin could trigger hostilities with the United States.

Let's assume that the Russians would avoid that confrontation, although they acutely resent American encroachment on their sphere of influence. What other options are there for

Russian intervention? They could try Afghanistan or Pakistan, where some Chechens and al Qaeda elements are holed up, or they could try Turkey. The United States is deeply involved in both Pakistan and Afghanistan. Turkey has a large Caucasian Muslim community—some say 10 percent of the total population—that dates from the nineteenth-century ethnic cleansing by Russia. Many still remain loyal to Chechnya. But Turkey is a member of NATO, and a Russian attack would trigger, yes, a run-in with the United States. Where else could Russia turn? Saudi Arabia? Yemen? The united States is fully engaged in both countries. What we are looking at is a possible conflict between Russia and the United States, as in the old Cold War days. Naturally, nobody in the news media has alerted Americans to the unfolding threat.

If the public knew more about the history and geography of troubled conflict zones like the Caucasus, perhaps it would take a stand in how America acts toward them, and how quickly our government moves to support our interests. The public might even take an interest in full-blown foreign wars such as Iraq before they happen, not necessarily to avoid them but at least to prosecute them intelligently—with the requisite geo-historical wisdom. Leave aside, for a moment, the controversial reasons the Bush administration gave for going in; leave aside also the inadequate diplomacy and troop strength. Just ask the question: Did anyone know enough of Iraq's history to prepare for this *particular* war? It's worth doing a brief thumbnail of Iraqi history just to see what the White House has gotten us into—keeping in mind that it's easier to win a war than an occupation in which internal conflicts plague any occupier not willing to suppress vast populations.

Up until the 1920s, the area now known as Iraq was ruled by the Ottoman Empire as a multi-ethnic, multi-faith patchwork of districts that also included the Gulf States such as Kuwait and Bahrain. It was never a whole or an entity, certainly not a country. The Ottomans lost it to the British in World War I, along with much of the Middle East. If you look at Iraq's oddly straight-line borders today, you will see that it's an essentially artificial space, invented by the British and designated a country. Like much of their Empire, they shaped it not out of an organic whole, but in such a way as to divide and rule the region easily—and above all, to include lots of newly discovered oil zones. To subdue the hostile population in the north, they used poison gas dropped from airplanes against both Kurds and Turcomans. So the British were the first to use WMD in Iraq—a bitter irony considering the U.S.-British excuse for invading and removing Saddam.

Until the 1920s, the Turcomans were simply Turks. But in order to separate them legally from Turkey, the British pretended that very few actual "Turks" lived in Iraq. The British then annexed the oil-rich northern zones of Kirkuk and Mosul illegally after the war, by inciting a Kurdish rebellion within Turkey to cause a distraction while they secured the "Turcoman" areas of Iraq. It's worth noting that the Turcoman/Turk gambit had been used before—notably by Lenin, as he subdued the Turkic republics of Central Asia, where he then forcibly taught its denizens their fictionalized tribal Turcoman heritage. The British did the same in Iraq; so did Saddam Hussein, in later years, until he changed his tack and started insisting that they all confess to being Arabs.

In the 1920s, the British imposed a king on Iraq from the Hashemite tribe that had previously ruled the Hijaz, now part of Saudi Arabia. The Brits had replaced the Hashemite dynasty with the Ibn Saud dynasty, thus creating Saudi Arabia. In compensation, the British gave Jordan to one Hashemite brother and Iraq to the other, both as custodians of British power. King Hussein of Jordan was a Hashemite, as is his son. Since the Brits had also unwisely championed the last (failed) Ottoman sultan against the nationalist regime of Attaturk in Turkey, former Ottoman court officials exiled from Turkey joined the British-Hashemites in Iraq. That Iraq lasted from the 1920s to the 1950s. When Iraq then had its own nationalist uprisings in the 1950s, the hastily composed polyglot royalist ruling class were all put to the sword or expelled. Nationalist, or Baathist, fever swept the larger Arab countries well into the mid-1960s—a wave of uprisings by young military officers from Egypt to Syria to Iraq, where Saddam Hussein ultimately won out. Saddam then proceeded to hold the country together through Stalinist tactics internally and by picking fights with neighboring countries.

All of which is to say that Iraq never was, and indeed never was intended to be, a real country that could hold together without force. In that respect Iraq is more like Yugoslavia than Afghanistan. Indeed, many Arabs assume that the United States intends to see Iraq break up in the long term. They see America's inordinate incompetence in stabliizing the country, the limited troop deployment, the unguarded borders, as part of an American strategy to let the country split apart deliberately while offering the merest pretense at trying to hold it together. Why would the United States do such a thing? Because three smaller oil-producing zones would be easier to control than an entire country the size of present-day Iraq.

Regardless of how you feel about the war, there's no reason not to assume that the Bush White House intended all along in good faith to pacify Iraq, much as it did Afghanistan. So why has that goal proven harder to effect in Iraq? For one thing, Afghanistan has existed in one form or another for centuries.

Its minorities have successfully shared power through tribal councils and coalitions for long periods. It has natural borders. Iraq, on the other hand, is an essentially artificial nation with porous borders, and in its short history one ethnic/religious group or other has dominated the rest—the same method of governance the United States is now employing there through military means. Most Americans don't know, for example, that the United States has used the Kurds as shock troops from the very beginning of the war. Kurdish troops or Peshmerga, as they are called, helped U.S. Special Forces subdue the Sunni triangle from the north while the regular body of U.S. troops came up from the south. Peshmerga featured heavily in post-Shock and Awe assaults on Fallujah and Najaf, that is, both in Sunni and Shi'ite arenas, which has had the effect of exacerbating ethnic tensions. More recently, when the Shi'ite leadership failed or refused to disarm the renegade Sadr militia of Muqtada Al-Sadr in the holy city of Najaf, the United States responded by threatening them implicitly with a revival of Sunni power. U.S. marines simply and suddenly withdrew from the Sunni stronghold of Fallujah (much against the wishes of the marines on the ground there). When the Shi'ite threat faded, the United States launched a hefty assault on the Sunni insurgents in Fallujah. So the coalition military has made full use of the internal tribal rivalries that the British built into Iraq.

Does that mean Iraq will never work as a democracy? Again, doesn't Afghanistan, itself riven with ethnic divisions, offer a positive example of a nation that seems to be making progress? Well, this is one case a little learning about history and geography can be a dangerous thing. When the American news media give you any context at all, it's often just enough to leave you half-informed and cocooned by your simplistic new assumptions. Iraq and Afghanistan *aren't* the same—why would they be? Or, to be more precise, they are similar in some ways and radically different in others. Afghanistan is a rural country; Iraq is a largely urban country—which makes for different kinds of wars. Afghanistan has always survived with a weak central government and strong provincial warlords; those who've attempted to alter the dynamic there by invasion—most notably the British and Soviet empires—have inevitably failed in the long term. To the degree that the United States has succeeded there, it has done so by letting warlords perpetuate their regional influence—perhaps unintentionally, certainly while pretending otherwise.

In Iraq, the United States has tried to use the Kurds as an equivalent to the Northern Alliance in Afghanistan—that is, as an ally that will help them forcibly subdue unrest and marginalize troublemakers while protecting the central government from being overthrown. The trouble is that what the Kurds really want is to secede from Iraq altogether, taking the oil-rich town of Kirkuk with them. They have no emotional loyalty to the concept of the Iraqi nation. From the early British years onward, they were corralled into the country forcibly and kept in it through violent suppression. Their leaders keep talking about Kirkuk being "the beating heart of Kurdistan." Even if the Kurds stay within a vaguely unified Iraq, unlike Afghanistan a decentralized or loosely federated Iraq may not remain stable for long. Its neighbors are simply not likely to permit it. The surrounding Sunni countries will want the Sunnis to have more power; the Iranians will try to influence the Shi'ites, while the Iraqi Shi'ites already want to dominate the entire country with their majority population numbers; and nobody wants the Kurds to have an oil-rich enclave that could be used to stir up trouble in Kurdish areas of Iran, Turkey, or Syria. Those countries want to nip Kurdish power in the bud by locking it down under a strong central Iraqi government. For all those reasons, too, a complete split into three parts wouldn't be likely to succeed: All the surrounding countries could be counted on to meddle in each component part indefinitely.

The United States, in short, has blundered into a hornet's nest. In the run-up to the war, the White House apparently made little effort to understand what Iraq was actually like underneath the Saddam façade—and the news media was no better. As I am writing this, in the fall of 2004, Iraq is suffering on average eighty violent incidents a day throughout the country, and not just in a few isolated places—and the news media is proving, if possible, even more inept in covering the country than ever. Only, by now, journalists simply cannot *physically* get around for fear of being kidnapped or killed. Kidnapping has moved from being a terrorist activity to doubling as a form of commerce operated by armed groups of unemployed locals in need of funds. (This was another direct result of American incompetence in disbanding the Iraqi army and most national industries, which left most Iraqi men unemployed.)

If we knew little about Iraq when we went in, it appears that we know still less and less as the days go by, with the disastrous result that our original misconceptions remain fixed in place. Ignorant of its history, impervious to its lethal geography, we even managed to misconstrue its current makeup. For the Pentagon and the White House, this may have been a failure of arrogance, or failed intelligence, or both; that will be debated for decades. But what about the press? Why did we drop the ball when it came to contemporary Iraq? One part of the answer was purely practical: Saddam prevented journalists from operating freely, and the embedded journalists in the war saw the country mostly through American gunsights. But there were other opportunities aplenty. From the time that Iraqis toppled Saddam's statue through roughly April 2004, journalists were able to operate with reasonable freedom around Iraq. Long before that—for some years before the war—journalists in vast numbers were also working in the northern Kurdish zone. Unfortunately, our historical ignorance led us to misinterpret a lot of what we saw; instead, all too often, we saw only what we wanted to see.

Take one central misconception that seems by now impossible to correct: that Iraq is made up simply of Sunnis, Shi'ites, and Kurds. As a thumbnail sketch of Iraq, this is close enough, perhaps, for the purpose of stirring up one side against another—but it's nowhere near a complex enough recipe to ensure a stable democracy there. And it's certainly not a full enough picture for an informed news media to consider responsible. The fact is some percentage of Shi'ites are not Arabs but Turcomans, a distinct group with their own language and customs. We don't know precisely how big the Turcoman Shi'ite population is, because Saddam's censuses were rigged and the United States still hasn't done a census, but the Turcomans themselves maintain that they constitute somewhere between 9 and 12 percent of the population, only a little less than the Kurds. For that matter, a good many Turcomans are also Sunni. So the Sunni-Shi'ite-Kurd triptych is already a dangerous simplification—and yet no one has paid the slightest attention to that distinction. Indeed, most journalists simply ignore the fact, depending on population numbers put out by others. And, in Iraq, rival power groups are all too happy to minimize each other's existence.

What about the Turcomans? What evidence can they offer to demonstrate their overlooked status? They point to census after census from even before Saddam's time to prove their claims. Saddam's efforts to forcibly integrate the Turcomans into the Arab population began in the 1970s: He rewarded Arabs for marrying Turcoman wives, rewarded Turcomans who chose to "become" Arab, and killed many who didn't. Thus, he managed to cook the census books—but it doesn't mean that Turcomans don't exist in the numbers they claim. And if they do, the makeup of Iraq becomes a darn sight more complicated than the old tripartite model would suggest . . . and the American blueprint for pacifying Iraq seems ever more crude and unpromising. So why hasn't this issue been addressed? Most simply, because it just complicates the received assumption that journalists lazily take on trust. But there are other reasons.

Nowhere has the news media's ignorant performance been more egregious than in its handling of the Kurds, a catalogue of sorry incompetence and dangerous misinformation that continues to this day. As mentioned, I have seen first-hand how CBS's New York headquarters rejected mention of the Kurds in reporting on Saddam's gas attacks against them on the grounds that Americans would find the reference too obscure. Another splendidly dismaying anecdote related by former first lady Barbara Bush[5] illustrates perfectly American public indifference to the complexities of Iraq. On a state visit to France, George H. W. Bush were riding with French president Francois Mitterand in one car, while the two first ladies were following in a second car. Mrs. Bush was feeling rather jetlagged and comfortable in the backseat, when Madame Mitterand launched into an impassioned lecture about the Kurds, a subject totally unfamiliar to Mrs. Bush. While Madame Mitterand regaled her guest with a mini-symposium on the problem, the American president's wife fell soundly asleep.

Such obliviousness wasn't the exclusive province of Mrs. Bush, of course. It was endemic enough to American observers—even those with real power in government, and certainly among the media—that once U.S. forces withdrew soon after the first Gulf War, Saddam was able to reinvade the northern Kurdish area and wreak damage at will with no American public outcry. Ultimately, of course, Americans in general, and U.S. policy in practice, did wake up to the Kurdish plight; the Iraqi Kurdish area prospered as a protected zone, and Kurds fight alongside U.S. forces to this day. All's well that ends well? Not quite.

The trouble is, once the American news media manage to conquer a tiny province of their own ignorance, they're reluctant to revisit the neighborhood anytime soon. By the time of the second Gulf War, the media had finally awakened to the existence of the Kurds in a highly positive way. Most halfway informed Americans now know, to some degree, who the Kurds are and what they've suffered. The Kurds are the good guys, the all–round perfect embodiment of victimhood and Saddam's cruelty. Their public image, thanks to our media, is that of a people full of admiration for America and yearning to be free. And, since they're now operating as our main local allies in Iraq, there's very little inclination to spotlight whatever negatives the Kurds might have—which, alas, are considerable.

Most Americans don't know, for example, that it was mainly the Kurds who looted much of the northern pipeline equipment in the early postwar period.[6] Their activities cost the United States dearly in dollars and time, critical time, before the pipelines could be restored. The Kurds looted much else besides, causing extensive damage in their early raids into the south during and after "Shock and Awe," but most of their bad deeds went unreported. *Wall Street Journal* correspondent Farnaz Fassihi recorded early reports of the Kurds' pillaging and violent attacks on civilians in the Sunni areas; the group played no small part in the spread of chaos and lawlessness during that critical period, for which the United States was widely blamed around the world; Kurdish borders with other countries became the main transit points for looted material out of Iraq. But the American press, indeed the western press as a whole, simply ignored that problem, and many others.

Why? Why miss such an important story? Several reasons, but they all boil down to a sorry excuse: the long-entrenched laziness of the media. The "enlightened" liberal world of the press regarded the Kurds for years as a textbook example of the oppressed third-world minority, especially as the Soviet Union championed their progaganda for years much as it did with the PLO and with Nelson Mandela's ANC. (The Kurds got no slack, of course, in idyllic socialist societies like Syria.) The Soviets turned a fractured tribal phenomenon into a liberation struggle for nationhood—again, much as they did with the PLO, the ANC, and many anti-imperialist movements in Africa. The fact that many of those movements reverted to their tribal components upon gaining power didn't dampen the enthusiasm of pro-Kurd national liberationists among European intellectuals, especially in France. Yet there were also plenty of liberal pro-Kurdish advocates at that time in the United States, Christopher Hitchens being one prominent example. On the right, the Kurds came into their own as the ideal anti-Saddam exhibit; for the Israelis, they offered a counterweight to the Arab bloc in the Middle East. The resulting flood of positive PR for the Kurds has poured unfiltered into the western press for years, from all quarters. At one point, a widespread news item even reported that the

Kurds themselves had played a crucial role in the capture of Saddam. American authorities denied the report firmly, yet Christopher Hitchens recorded it as a fact in his column for the online journal *Slate*. That same day, the BBC revealed that one of Saddam's bodyguards had given him up in order to claim the reward for his capture.

All these Kurd-friendly influences came together in the weeks leading up to the Iraq invasion, when the northern Kurdish zone was teeming with western journalists. Unfortunately, virtually none of them spoke local languages. All outside journalists had to be officially accredited to stay in the region—and once accredited they were obliged to work with appointed Kurdish interpreters or guides, a provision explained by Kurdish authorities as necessary for journalists' security. Where have we heard that before? In virtually every police state, for starters. Astonishingly, no journalists questioned the arrangement. As a result, the world heard nothing of the tribulations and suffering of minorities like the Turcomans and the Assyrian Christians, who had to live under the strong arm of Kurdish rule after suffering acutely for years under Saddam. Nor did we learn much about the extreme and longstanding animosity between the two Kurdish factions, the PUK under Jalal Talebani and the KDP under Massoud Barzani. During the Iran-Iraq war, Talebani had collaborated with the Iranians—the real reason that his side of Kurdistan was gassed by Saddam at a time when it was virtually Iranian territory. Still, the Iranian side almost won; Barzani was losing the civil war until he joined forces with Saddam and reinvaded his region in 1996 with the Iraqi 10th Army, recapturing his capital of Erbil from the opposing Kurdish-Iranian faction. Then he handed over to Saddam's torturers leaders of the Assyrian and Turcoman communities. None returned alive.

As America geared up for the 2003 invasion, those memories remained fresh for those minorities. The harassment of leaders, ransacking of party offices, anonymous attacks on community centers all continued. But none of this got reported to the world in the pre-invasion period, even though there were plenty of top media organs camped out in Kurdistan. And here comes the most reprehensible part: the news organizations were obliged to hold their tongues largely for fear of offending the Kurdish authorities, which could have won them expulsion. They had all invested massively in covering the upcoming war; they could not risk being thrown out.

Even those journalists who wanted to know what went on in the Kurdish zone generally didn't, because their Kurdish guides managed their access to information. CNN lived in a compound unto itself, with ten SUVs and a dozen armed Kurdish minders in the compound. They had no interest in peering behind the curtain of Kurdish rule. Having been thrown out of Baghdad, they couldn't risk the same in Erbil. Fox News was no different—probably much worse, considering their rah-rah support of the war. If Fox News knows one thing above all, it knows not to confuse America with too much nuance. Once the war started, at least, CNN got free of their minders and did very well. (They have two top Middle East correspondents, based in Beirut and Cairo respectively, who understand the region well.) At one point, while covering the chaos of Iraq's liberation in the North they openly told viewers that Kurdish hangers-on were threatening and beating back Arabs who wanted to tell them of Kurdish brutality.

Americans might be entitled to ask: Why does such detail matter to them? Isn't it too "inside baseball," as it were, to matter in a real way to American audiences? Well, no, it's not. The Kurdish question matters because how the Kurds behave towards others will determine whether Iraq sinks into civil war . . . and, thus, whether Iraq stays whole. It matters because the United States allowed the Kurds to take over all of Saddam's heavy weaponry in the north—against all previously given guarantees that no such thing would happen. And, critically, it matters because of the fate of the strategically critical city of Kirkuk.

In the wake of the invasion, the United States allowed the Kurds to take over the strategic oil towns of Kirkuk and Mosul, against all previous assurances. The Kurds were promptly thrown out of Mosul by fierce armed resistance, but continued to occupy Kirkuk and slowly annex it with a heavy population influx from Kurdistan. They argue, in part correctly, that they were merely returning to homes from which Saddam had purged the years before. But now, having forcibly seized civic control of the Kirkuk area—including its land deeds office, where they burned many documents to hide original land ownership records—the Kurds are busily creating "facts on the ground" in the time-honored Israeli fashion. Every day, while controlling who else comes in, they return to Kirkuk in such large numbers that they will soon change the population balance. In the meantime, the United States postpones the population census of Iraq. The other minorities believe that by the time the census happens, the change in population balance will justify Kirkuk's absorption into the Kurdish zone. They also believe that the process is a precursor for allowing the division of Iraq into three separate zones of Shi'ites, Sunnis, and Kurds, with the Kurds getting oil-rich Kirkuk to make them financially viable. If it survives, an independent Kurdistan with oil from Kirkuk could resemble a Gulf State such as Kuwait or Oman—with the added attribute of being non-Arab. It would start out life as a kind of protectorate or western client state, as indeed did the Gulf States, but it would also be most useful as a kind strategic irritant to nearby Syria and Iran. One can see the attraction of that outcome for the United States.

But it won't be easy to pull off such a feat—because of the outside hostility I've noted, and because the internal enmities in the area already point to civil strife. Kirkuk's other resident ethnic groups, the Turcomans and Assyrians and Arabs, have already suffered Kurdish massacres of civilians and have armed themselves in response. The city faces the kind of internecine tensions that might yet engulf all of Iraq. So the Kurds may not, after all, be the ideal trouble-free allies for America to embrace publicly, or for the world to continue to champion as perennial victims. All of this matters because it makes the job of pacifying Iraq that much harder. And, finally, it matters because the Kurds will be the ones to suffer if the allies blink or lose interest again, as they did after the Gulf War, when the United States withdrew and left the Kurds to suffer Saddam's ire for more than a decade. This time, everyone will jump on the Kurds—for allying with Israel, for attacking other Iraqis, for depending exclusively on American backing while alienating all their neighbors. And, as usual, Americans back home will wonder why it all happened.

Yet, nobody in the American news media wants to burden us with such complex and challenging details. You never know what might happen—viewers might switch to another channel.

By now Americans know, or should know, that ethnic groups who have historical grievances—those who have suffered oppression, massacres, or genocidal wars—can carry a sense of victimhood for generations. Many of the world's trouble spots boil over as a result of precisely such history. Victimhood can soon turn into revenge. And the news media do a very erratic job of informing Americans evenhandedly about such matters. Getting sufficient publicity for past suffering becomes a crucial propaganda strategy for rival national groups, because it can justify all kinds of preemptive measures against others. And so those who fail to win publicity usually lose the ensuing war.

The Chechens, for example, have utterly failed to convey their suffering to the world. To the world, the outrages they commit appear to be just that—mere barbaric behavior. Indeed, the Russians have successfully portrayed themselves as the victims in their genocidal wars against the Chechens. The Serbs, too, lost the propaganda war in the end, though they succeeded long enough to grab and keep much of the land they wanted (excluding Kosovo). The Serbs believed that in attacking Bosnian Muslims they were redressing historical grievances going back half a millennium. In attacking the Croats, they were redressing more recent wrongs dating back to World War II, when the Croats had worked with the Nazis to dominate the Serbs. The same victim-turned-oppressor dynamic applied in Rwanda, where the Hutus slaughtered the Tutsis because the Tutsis had repressed them for a century or more with western help. The Hutus never tried to show the world their suffering in order to explain their grievances against Tutsis. Despite having endured massacres and domination for a century, they turned on their former masters in full view of world cameras; as a result they are now identified, for all time, as genocidal maniacs. Once publicly established, victimhood can furnish a shield against criticism. But without that vaccination, the victors in any civil war can look like unprovoked barbarians. As usual, American mass news media, especially television news, offers very little depth or impartiality in covering such events.

One reason for this is the visceral power of television as a visual medium. When TV cameras show human rights outrages, the visual effect simply blows away all political debate. Thus the Russians have effectively precluded all western TV coverage of Chechnya by simply allowing journalists to be killed or kidnapped in the war zone, while blaming everything on Chechen bandits. In Iraq, it's not clear who currently benefits from the increased absence of western cameras. Abu Ghraib aside, Americans have seen little footage of local victims of U.S. operations—a constant complaint by Arab media commentators. But one can certainly say the Kurds have clearly benefited from the aggregate imbalance of coverage, since we see little evidence of their operations either. In a country seething with group grievances, the Kurds remain the designated victims while everyone else nurses the wounds of their victimhood . . . while waiting, no doubt, for a future opportunity to hit back.

All of which may sound far too elaborate for average Americans to absorb. But merely to accept that kind of ignorance as a fact of life means accepting a creeping end to informed democracy in our country. It means letting the government operate beyond our shores without our full knowledge, and facing a world that increasingly hates us, both for what is done abroad in our name and for our complacent insularity. It means effectively allowing interested lobbies to run areas of foreign policy without our consent. It ultimately means more 9/11 disasters without warning. After all, would any of this really seem too complicated if one really believed that one's survival depended on it? If Americans can take on rafts of nuanced data about their favorite celebrities, speculate on how many pounds Oprah has gained or lost, whether Janet Jackson sports breast implants, or which reality show is number one, why can't they follow the history and geography of a dangerous world, one that could lash back and violently end their insularity without warning?

Americans must know more and ask more about what's going on abroad—from their government, from each other, and especially from the media. As American-based British historian Niall Ferguson argues in his recent book *Colossus,* the United States runs a kind of world empire, without acknowledging the fact to itself and without shouldering the onus that goes with it.[7] The bottom line: We have vital interests abroad, and in a democracy we must know about those interests, consent in them, monitor and defend them. Otherwise, we let the various hidden oligarchies in our body politic implicate us all in their doings abroad.

This, ultimately, is the job of the news media. And they are failing us dangerously.

CHAPTER EIGHT

WHERE HAVE THEY GONE, THE GREAT FOREIGN CORRESPONDENTS?

T he greatest moments of reporting from abroad seem to occur during wars, or so we often think in hindsight, especially when the events directly affect America—and not just because it matters more to us. Correspondents can rise to the occasion and do great work, but their work also allows us to feel the entire nation listening or watching with us like an audience in a theater. When the danger and exhaustion can be felt in the broadcast, and correspondents become so immersed in the drama that history speaks through them, stars are born and memories are fixed to their performance.

Edward R. Murrow's haunting radio transmissions during the London blitz in World War II marked perhaps the first great foreign broadcasting triumph from a war zone. That war also produced the most celebrated everyman journalist figure in Ernie Pyle, the definitive embedded reporter, who lived with GIs and wrote of their daily lives for the now defunct Scripps-Howard newspapers. Our industry continued to score such popular triumphs in the public memory through the decades—even into the first Gulf War, when CNN correspondents worked virtually around the clock from the famous Al Rasheed Hotel in Baghdad covering the pyrotechnics of American smart bombing around them. Their ordeal became the movie *Live from Baghdad,* based on the memoir of CNN producer Robert Weiner. Even in Vietnam, despite (or because of) the controversial stance of many correspondents in opposing the war, Americans knew and valued their individual contributions.

Suddenly, though, we no longer produce foreign correspondents with the popular following and public trust of former times. What happened? Where, in short, have all the Ernie Pyles gone?

Think back to the coverage of Afghanistan and Iraq of the past four years—conflicts that should be freshest in your mind. For you, which correspondents stamped their names on those dramas? Is there anyone working today who has successfully gained the stature and authority to become our eyes and ears, our trusted guide to those perplexed war zones? Sadly, the question applies more to broadcast than to print, simply because print media did a much better job of in-depth of reporting on Iraq and Afghanistan. John Burns of the *New York Times* and Seymour Hersh of *The New Yorker* come to mind: both veteran journalists, with long records of previous outstanding work, reminded us of that extraordinary sensation where you know, however briefly, that you're witnessing a deep shaft of light onto the truth. It was Seymour Hersh who published the Abu Ghraib material at the same time as *60 Minutes*; both had been working on the story independently. John Burns, a two-time Pulitzer win-

ner, has stood out for his comprehensive and candid reporting from Baghdad since the United States bombing began in
March 2003. After the war, Burns expressed his disdain for
reporters who had sucked up to the Ministry of Information
in order to gain or maintain access while Saddam Hussein
was still in power.[1] Can you cite similar work by American
TV foreign correspondents?

Sure, Iraq is a tough and dangerous environment to work
in. But that's our job—and correspondents from other countries manage it. One reporter for the French national channel
France 2 spent most of September 2004 living in Fallujah and
showing a face of the war Americans almost never see. Visiting nonpartisan innocent citizens of the notorious Sunni
stronghold, he showed how they survived by digging cellars to
live in during American aerial bombing attacks, how they sub-
sisted on little food, and feared for their children. American
channels could have picked up the material for rebroadcast
stateside, but none did. Now why would that be? One specu-
lative answer: reluctant to leave the comparative safety of their
hotels in Baghdad, American TV teams wouldn't have been
eager to showcase correspondents from other countries who
were doing a better job. I know few American correspondents
who would be willing to risk their lives to show a sympathetic
picture of Iraqis under siege by American forces.

In fact, few of my American network colleagues are now
willing even to go to Iraq. NBC News correspondent Jim
Maceda estimates that an American television correspondent
is worth at least four million dollars to the kidnappers who
capture westerners and hold them for ransom or sell them to
the highest bidders.[2] Maceda says his NBC News bosses in
New York "talk every day about whether we should stay."
Other television news organizations express similar reservations. Most American correspondents now find covering Iraq

both dangerous and unrewarding. "If you are not embedded," Maceda says, "you cannot cover the war. Going to the Green Zone [the sealed off administrative center of Baghdad] to a press conference takes up most of your day and nervous energy. At the hotel, you don't talk to hotel staff. You try to conceal your movements."

This fear of the unknown has always been a challenge for foreign correspondents. Yet, the greatest correspondents of the past have overcome it repeatedly. Why do we need to keep learning that lesson? In one hypnotic segment from the celebrated 1972 Vietnam documentary *Hearts and Minds,* a recently freed American prisoner, a lieutenant, addresses a junior high school after coming home—and tells the kids, in effect, that Vietnam is a great place except for the local people, who "make a mess of everything."

One journalist friend of mine told me a story of approaching Sheila Nevins, the head of HBO documentaries, at the outset of the Afghan campaign, to propose going on location early to live with the locals and see how the war affected them. Nevins dismissed the idea, saying that she "didn't want to know about those awful people," and had no interest in "what they're like." What she preferred was a picture of American soldiers—boys and girls from the neighborhoods of the heartland—living and suffering and fighting. Nothing wrong with that, of course—except for what it reflected about American audiences' resistance to anything alien or beyond their ken. Unfortunately, American soldiers can't do that. How about showing folks back home what our soldiers might be up against? Or how about showing us which of "those awful people" are the enemy and which are not? According to my friend, Nevins illustrates the kind of consistently successful executive who got to the top, like many others, by divining the entrenched popular tastes of mainstream America, not by asking anyone to think beyond their limits. Her kind of television doesn't need foreign correspondents.

I've gone into some detail in previous chapters about the reasons for deteriorating American news, particularly on television. The news industry's downward arc almost exactly parallels that of the foreign correspondent: It happened during the 1990s, and mostly for the same reasons, including underfunding, arrogant insularity, contempt for the viewer's attention span, loss of mission, corporate greed, the collusion between corporate power, and a spineless FCC. What happened to foreign correspondents, in short, was mostly done *to* them.

But they must also shoulder some of the blame. After all, many of these damaging trends were things the journalists more or less allowed to happen, and during a time when they weren't exactly invisible or voiceless. The foreign correspondents never thought to fight back for their share of the market. They didn't rouse themselves to lobby for their function publicly by appealing directly to Americans or by shaming their bosses. If they had truly believed that theirs was a sacred public trust and that their work directly impacted the lives and safety of the public, you'd think that foreign correspondents would be fighting mad over what has happened to them. If so, where's the heat? Where's the stridency?

I don't exclude myself in this apathetic story. In the 1990s, we all grew conditioned to a life of receiving marching orders and leaping off at a moment's notice into volatile zones, doing our best to scrape away at the mine face of news, often in conditions of great adversity; that's already a sizeable workload. It never occurred to us that we might have to fight for the integrity of our vocation, too. It may be, too, that we were suffering from moral battle fatigue. As *Nightline*'s Tom Bettag says, "I think people have just been worn down. The old guard that believes in this stuff has fought and fought so many times that they have just been worn down on it in general. And the younger people just don't believe that anything can be done." In the end, though, we must—because it's not a fight for ourselves but for our country's safety, and we haven't done it effectively, if at all.

We failed in other ways, too—among other things, by bringing upon ourselves accusations of political bias that were too often justified. After Vietnam, many in our profession took to doubting the use of American force anywhere at any time. Even today, third-world populist strongmen, like Hugo Chavez in Venezuela, merely have to invoke America's role as a bully (while cozying up to Fidel Castro) to get a free pass from American media criticism. For similar reasons, President Reagan's active assault on Soviet power faced nothing but unremitting opposition from the American news media throughout the 1980s.

We all got caught up in this sort of liberal groupthink. I remember covering Reagan's 1987 speech in Berlin when he issued his dramatic challenge, "Mr. Gorbachev, tear down this wall." At the time, I thought it was just right-wing rhetoric. Why did the war against the marxist Sandinistas in Nicaragua have to be funded illegally through the Iran-Contra scheme? Because both Congress and the press viewed American power as more dangerous than leftist revolutions. Remember the issue of "moral equivalency," where critics on the right argued that the press were wrong to insist on taking a middle position between America and its enemies? The critics had a point. We had lost perspective on our own biases. How could Americans trust our reports from left-right war zones in Africa or Latin America if we invariably saw the opposition as champions of the people?

After the demise of Jimmy Carter's malaise-ridden presidency, the mood at home changed throughout the 1980s. The tenor of our news media, however, remained stuck in a political rut. As Vietnam-era thinking increasingly diverged from contemporary challenges, the industry's sense of impartiality looked outdated and partisan toward the left. In the 1970s, Carter's weakness had led to Soviet expansion, the invasion of Afghanistan, and the taking of the American embassy hostages in Iran. The Reagan era promised a recovery of American power and self-confidence; the public felt the results, but the news media droned on imperviously about inequities at home and American injustices abroad—that *was* the hard news of the day, or so we thought.

The average American recognized something that we foreign correspondents may have lost touch with: that other countries had worse problems than we did, and that many of them behaved far worse on the world stage than we did. To many viewers (a few of whom, of course, became highly influential conservative commentators themselves), the news was simply an excuse for liberal whining and Vietnam-era guilt. Eventually, middle America turned away from such incessant self-flagellation. As commerce replaced hard news in the mainstream media, the public hardly objected to cutbacks in the news or the dwindling number (or quality) of the networks' foreign correspondents. They simply filled the void with material they preferred: Christian broadcasting, Rush Limbaugh, Fox News and the like.

But let's not imagine that the result represents a better news industry, by any stretch. These newcomers represent even more pre-programmed newsmongering, all of it prescribed by a rigid agenda. The news gets pre-selected to fit the political message. The home office rules over its correspondents, requiring them to acknowledge only the news that fits their vision of the world. Nothing unexpected seeps through—and with each passing year the correspondent loses even more authority and traction. It was this loss of authority, over time, that led to a world in which our warnings about the rising threat of Islamic terror abroad went unheeded. And a world in which President Bush could impugn our patriotism and outvoice us as he pushed forward with his Iraq invasion, the trumpets of the conservative media at his back. By the time election time came around, President Bush had learned that he could implicitly dismiss all negative media reports from Iraq simply by asserting that "freedom is on the march"—and no serious public outcry would follow.

In a free-market system like ours, where glamour follows money, the job of foreign correspondent lost glamour as the function got defunded and power moved away to other jobs in the profession. Foreign correspondents are "very hard to recruit," as Peter Jennings observes. "They are told, first of all, it's not the hottest thing. It's not the way to get to the top." Sure, there are still some young tyros who line up to volunteer for the job, but many change their minds soon enough when faced with kidnappings, threats, and unresponsive bosses. Many others regard it as merely a stepping stone to fast-track positions back home interviewing Martha Stewart or covering the grand self-centered "reality show" that is America. These days, very few who start out covering subjects abroad stay the course long enough to make a life of it.

Think of it: Besides Christiane Amanpour, how many names come to mind when you think of foreign correspondents? As Lawrence Grossman, former president of NBC News, says, "It used to that everybody knew the major correspondents. They were household names. Collingwood[3] and the others. Nobody knows anybody now who is doing the reporting. They have no identity, because they hardly ever show up on the air." The public itself wonders about the psychology of anyone who would choose to spend time in a place like Iraq. Those who do often face the accusation that they must be "adrenaline junkies" with a self-destructive streak. "Why on earth do you do it?" is a common refrain from friends and peers, once a correspondent gets old enough to have a family and kids. This is one concern that hasn't affected me much—I lived through the profession's golden years—but I can see what happens around me: My younger colleagues now carry (or fear they carry) the kind of faint social stigma that attaches to those who didn't have the smarts to enter Wall Street or Hollywood; they exist under the same cloud as, say, a Peace Corps volunteer. Of course, such a mindset is very much a holdover from our pre-9/11 fool's paradise. Foreign correspondents arguably matter now more than ever, as for the first time our country faces a drawn-out struggle against enemies who might actually use nuclear devices against us if they could—without the deterrence of assured massive retaliation. Indeed, there's evidence that the jihadists would invite such a conflagration, as part of their strategic plan to provoke a world war between Islam and the west. Any committed professional who would dare to foray into their lairs and bring back knowledge of the enemy should be showered with applause and celebrated, not belittled, by peers and viewers alike.

All of which may sound like portentous fear-mongering, end-of-the-world-as-we-know-it stuff. In more precise terms, then, what is it exactly that we lose in news coverage when our foreign correspondents lose stature and support? Let's take a concrete instance: the Tora Bora campaign in Afghanistan, during which al Qaeda cadres withdrew into mountain caves while the American command turned over much of the ground campaign to local proxies who were supported by laser-guided munitions from U.S. air power. There were various correspondents covering the action, but they came and went throughout the campaign. Most had no experience of Afghanistan or any sense of Afghan society—among them the ubiquitous Geraldo, who entered the war theater with a noisy flourish for Fox News, a massive retinue of local bodyguards and support staff at his back, and advertised his heroism when a bullet richocheted somewhere in the vicinity. Like everyone else, Geraldo watched the action from several hilltops away; he had no idea of real events on the battlefield. The outcome of that last stand by al Qaeda in Tora Bora later became an issue in the 2004 election, as John Kerry accused President Bush of letting Osama bin Laden escape by using local troops instead of well-trained, highly committed American troops. Vice President Cheney called that accusation "absolute garbage" in a stump speech in Ohio quoted on the White House web site on October 19, 2004. In support of his point, he cited the view of General Tommy Franks—who had run both the Afghan and the Iraq "Shock and Awe" campaigns. So which side was telling us the truth? In fact, as various weblogs have noted, a *Washington Post* article soon after Tora Bora from April 17, 2002, opened with the lead:

> The Bush administration has concluded that Osama bin Laden was present during the battle for Tora Bora late last year and that failure to commit U.S. ground troops to hunt him was its gravest error in the war against al Qaeda, according to civilian and military officials with first-hand knowledge.

During the election campaign, Mr. Cheney *et al.* also began to cast doubt on whether Osama bin Laden had been there at all.

The intelligence was sketchy, they claimed; it was all mere speculation. Yet, the same *Washington Post* article from 2002 had pointed out:

> Intelligence officials have assembled what they believe to be decisive evidence, from contemporary and subsequent interrogations and intercepted communications, that bin Laden began the battle of Tora Bora inside the cave complex along Afghanistan's mountainous eastern border.

On the matter of miscalculating by using local troops instead of committed American troops, the *Post* continued:

> After-action reviews, conducted privately inside and outside the military chain of command, describe the episode as a significant defeat for the United States. A common view among those interviewed outside the U.S. Central Command is that Army Gen. Tommy R. Franks, the war's operational commander, misjudged the interests of putative Afghan allies and let pass the best chance to capture or kill al Qaeda's leader. Without professing second thoughts about Tora Bora, Franks has changed his approach fundamentally in subsequent battles, using Americans on the ground as first-line combat units. In the fight for Tora Bora, corrupt local militias did not live up to promises to seal off the mountain redoubt, and some colluded in the escape of fleeing al Qaeda fighters. Franks did not perceive the setbacks soon enough, some officials said, because he ran the war from Tampa with no commander on the scene above the rank of lieutenant colonel. The first Americans did not arrive until three days into the fighting. "No one had the big picture," one defense official said.

The point of highlighting this pronounced disagreement isn't simply to offer one more instance of Bush White House spin or of election-time mendacity. The web universe now monitors such things with great efficiency, as candidates have repeatedly found to their cost. But the web universe, as everyone knows, comprises a highly partisan environment, in which bloggers generally preach to their own converted.

Which is where the old authoritative voice of the experienced, impartial, trusted foreign correspondent comes in. No he-said-she-said dispute could outweigh the reporting of Murrow in Britain, or Cronkite in Vietnam or the CNN team in Baghdad during the first Gulf War. They knew their terrain, and the public trusted their expertise. No politician would have attempted a revisionist gloss of what they had unveiled to the world. Authoritative foreign correspondents offer a natural antidote to spin, but America could provide no such figures in Afghanistan—not the way other countries did. The BBC, for example, had John Simpson, their World Affairs Editor and a veteran of years of reporting on Afghanistan. He was ably guided by the legendary Peter Jouvenal, the leading producer/cameraman in the region, who has covered the area since the invasion and expulsion of the Soviets. Jouvenal speaks local languages; he knows the players, and has stayed with the subject for decades. Such experience shamed almost anything available in the American news media, which had virtually refused to cover Afghanistan from the time of the Soviet withdrawal.

Anyone familiar with Afghan habits would know that almost all sieges there end with corrupt agreements between warring parties. Warlords know they have to live with each other afterward, and the exchange of payoffs is the price of any temporary detente. From the outset of the campaign, town after town swiftly fell to pro-American Northern Alliance troops precisely because Taliban fighters were allowed to leave after a deal was struck. On one notorious occasion, the Pakistani military even had the leisure to fly in troop carriers and lift out their advisors from a besieged town—advisors who had worked with Taliban and al Qaeda elements. Indeed, a number of American critics wondered who else they'd taken with them, and why the United States, which controlled Afghan skies, had allowed the airlift. By the time Tora Bora happened, everyone involved should have known that Afghan militia fighting with the American coalition would not change their time-honored habits—and they didn't. Indeed, many old-time veterans (Peter Jouvenal among them) assumed that America was deliberately using local proxies to drive the opposition out more quickly through wily deals, because in that terrain one couldn't hope to kill them all. Result? They had to be neutralized at a later date, by fair means or foul. Most informed observers realized that the United States had merely postponed the reckoning. So bin Laden's escape surprised no one. But the lack of a trusted voice, of a veteran foreign correspondent literate in Afghan affairs explaining such things nightly to American viewers—left average Americans with no serious guide to the war, nobody to put it all together for them. As the defense official said, "No one had the big picture." And as a result, come election time two years later, politicians could spin the events any which way they liked.

A foreign correspondent's utility can be boiled down to three practical functions: seeing the events, filtering the important parts down to news, and infusing a point of view where necessary. But all three gel into something greater than the sum of their parts when the correspondent's own judgment helps to shape the message as it's delivered. Without that, the rest can be outsourced separately and the job finished in the studio—which is the growing, and discouraging, trend within the industry. As small, handheld DVD cams become more available worldwide, the job of seeing can fall to stringers and freelances who happen to occupy the spot where a news event happens: a flood, a volcano, even a massacre. The footage those stringers send in gets sold on through various agencies to our news channels. The studio in London or New York sifts through the available incoming material to decide what makes news. And then they add studio experts to comment on—or read their reports over—the relevant parts. There you have it: a cheap, efficient operation, which to the average viewer can look for all the world like a real news broadcast.

Naturally, with such a process one must overlook a few minor shortcomings. What if no local witness happens to record, say, a massacre of Chechens by Russian soldiers? What if the Russians won't allow anyone into the area even to hear about the incident? That sort of thing happens all the time. In the absence of a resident correspondent, no one is on hand to argue for the event's significance to the news boss back home . . . and the story likely goes unreported and unnoticed. The Russian barbarism continues, and the Chechens resort to equal barbarism in return. And Americans never realize that their gas prices are rising because Russia has put a choke on its oil-rich neo-colonies.

In a serious environment, where news-gathering isn't aping Wal-Mart in its race to the bottom line, where news doesn't have to insulate viewers in a feelgood fantasy just to sell commercials, channels would invest long-term in foreign bureaus and correspondents. They would, in effect, be investing in the correspondent's growing experience, judgment, and foresight. That is what they pay for—when they do pay. In the past, network news division gave their future anchors plenty of years in the field to give them credibility. Sadly, as Peter Jennings points out, they have discontinued the practice.

"This is a dilemma I think the next generation of anchor people are going to have—Brian Williams, and whoever does it for us or with CBS: they have not been given the privileges that our companies gave us, of saying, *You are a long-term investment here, Jennings,* or Koppel, or Rather, *and you are going to do five years here, and two years here, and five years here. You might face twenty years [as a correspondent]."* Audiences have certainly responded to that kind of experience in past decades; why not now? Instead, during the recent Afghan/Iraq conflicts, we saw a lot of studio-based experts, especially on cable news. And though they cost a lot less than correspondents, such paid experts hardly provide an adequate substitute for real journalism. As in criminal trials, there are experts who will say anything for a paycheck. At a time when news channels stand accused of political bias on a daily basis, their use of hired experts offering opinion and comment in place of news seems like an unwise choice. Ideally, the correspondent embodies independent judgment in the face of home office executives—like an intelligence chief reporting to the executive branch. In neither case should bosses determine what gets reported for political reasons, as the Bush White House evidently did when they went out to select intelligence for a *casus belli* against Iraq.

In a properly run news operation, correspondents in the field don't act as mouthpieces for a coordinated network editorial policy. They don't set out to find what the home office wants them to find. Their information and judgment should determine editorial policy. That's what the Murrows and Cronkites did, and the public heeded them in their millions.

Sadly, today foreign correspondents are losing their individual identities slowly but surely to the predetermined political and commercial needs of their news channels. They're essentially bought-and-paid-for opiners standing on location to share the company biases from a picturesque locale for a day or two. Ideally, the point of foreign correspondence is for journalists to make informed judgments after immersing themselves in the actual place—unlike the home-studio experts, who are often chosen based on what the public's mood can take, or what the *New York Times* or leading opinion makers are saying that day. News channels understand the difference in value between studio experts and correspondents perfectly. That's why they all have bureaus and correspondents in the nation's capital. They don't believe foreign bureaus are any less important; they just won't pay for them.

Perhaps the strongest argument for foreign correspondents is that, at their best, they have a *strategic overview* of world affairs. They know how small incidents abroad weave together to affect American interests in the broader picture. That may sound a little counterintuitive; after all, shouldn't the news boss back home—whose position is closer to that of a general than a GI—have a better understanding of the total picture? Sadly, the industry has weakened too far for that. The home boss is usually preoccupied with the ratings war, and couldn't care less about a strategic anything abroad. It's the foreign correspondent who best knows, for example, that high oil prices may negatively affect Americans stateside—but may benefit American strategic interests by keeping Russia stable, Venezuela quiet and Iraq more viable. Reporting from such a large coherent perspective puts reporters on a great arching world stage; it also elevates their stature in the public's eyes.

Unquestionably, the Cold War furnished such a grand theater for the correspondents who covered it. In those days, Americans were instantly able to picture a vast Manichean world divide, and place the correspondent's location on it with a tacit knowledge of what it meant to themselves. A report from the obscurity of Brest-Litovsk, for instance, meant a glimpse deep inside the great enemy's terrain; for many viewers, such a report brought the world map instinctively into focus. They didn't have to argue for their report's relevance either to the boss or to viewers—never a dignified activity. These days, outside the Middle East, each miserable conflict erupts and wanes in isolation; a correspondent's report on the situation is likely to seem meager and disconnected. And the tragedy lies not in the damage to our profession, but in our profession's resulting inability to serve the public.

As ever, one man's loss is another's opportunity. Foreign correspondents haven't disappeared altogether, and anyone with the merest enterprise can have a field day cherry-picking gigantic unreported stories. As Seymour Hersh told a German journalist, he couldn't believe the overlooked opportunities he could snap up simply because *The New Yorker* allowed him to write what he wanted. Having already uncovered numerous scandals, from Abu Ghraib to the controversial Israeli-Kurdish alliance in Iraq (both hidden in plain sight for anyone to pick up), Hersh cited two future possibilities for investigation, including the background of interim Iraqi Prime Minister Allawi and prisoner abuse at Guantanamo; he would go on to cover them in more depth in his recent book *Chain of Command*.[4] Now why, you might wonder, would Hersh give away his intentions? Won't someone else come along and scoop him? Sadly, the answer seems to be *no*. Those stories have indeed knocked around at the edges of news consciousness for some time, yet no one before Hersh had put much energy into exploring them. Few American correspondents have the freedom to take the lead, and even fewer have the authority to make a topic important just by choosing it. Human Rights Watch, a leading international human rights monitoring outfit, has complained about prisoner abuses in Guantanamo since 2003, but no one paid much heed until Abu Ghraib, when the generic issue of Geneva Conventions and POW legal protections got aired. Yet even then, as Hersh discovered, Guantanamo still escaped full scrutiny.

As for interim prime minister Allawi, a number of foreign newsgroups had scrutinized his past history, but their American counterparts didn't think to make an issue of it. No doubt many considered the topic too obscure or complicated for the American public; others probably thought they would be branded as unpatriotic for taking on the issue. And what were they missing? It turns out that Allawi was a close confidante of Saddam for many years, until they fell out for reasons that remain unclear. Allawi made it to the west, lived in London, and seems to have worked with the CIA and Iraqi exile groups that appear to have been implicated in anti-Saddam terrorist acts, such as bombings in public places in Baghdad, in which innocents died. This was the man appointed by the United States to take Iraq into its first democratic national election. With no Cronkites or Murrows to explore such a figure, it was left to the rare standout like Sy Hersh to do the spadework.

Hersh is right to say that our news organizations leave enormously important news topics untouched, even though our profession knows enough to pursue them. The fact is, those foreign correspondents who do know about such things generally don't have the in-house power to do much about it— and those who have the power don't know enough about what there is to cover. You can talk till you're blue in the face to the executive producer for nightly news about the importance of an overlooked topic, but ultimately his job is to run a kind of triage operation. To some degree, he trusts in the natural selectivity of ignorance. If America, the consumer, has resisted being informed on topic X, the topic must be at fault. America's ignorance has more authority than the foreign correspondent. Such are the perils of treating news as a commodity. A few correspondents, those who've known higher standards at other times, still retain a sense of public trust—that the public deserves to know what it doesn't want to know . . . yet. The eighteenth-century British statesman Edmund Burke famously noted that his constituents had elected him to exercise his judgment, not to base each decision on its potential popularity; he rejected the validity of a rolling referendum on his actions for the same reason that the news world should be wary of living by minute-by-minute ratings.

Readers, take heart: I am not advocating a return to "serious" foreign news in the style of the post-Vietnam years, with their relentless, guilt-inflected litany of war, famine, and disaster. This is no Victorian recipe for virtuous seriousness—that anything that hurts, tastes bad, or bores you must be good for the soul. But who says the alternative to gloom and doom has to be news that competes with *Celebrity Blackjack* or *elimiDATE* or reality TV? Americans merely need to be informed about how each foreign story affects them directly, and why, in each case, they should be paying close attention. As it is, more and more immigrant Americans, first generation or beyond, vote for the candidate who best upholds the interests of their old ethnic country of origin. Before the 2004 election, the Internet was abuzz with expatriate newsgroups judging the candidates by such single-issue criteria. Consider that such groups invariably maintain financial ties with their ethnic country, and the implications get clearer. American elections have become elections that affect the world, and which the world tries to influence. We may not like the idea—we certainly don't debate it enough—but America's virtually open borders have created a slippery continuum between us and the world, with people, money, deals, and political pressure flowing back and forth with abandon. Only mainstream Americans are kept out of the loop.

For all these reasons, the foreign correspondent should be enjoying a professional heyday. More than ever, our country is part of "abroad." America should be fighting its news industry for the reempowerment of foreign correspondents; the correspondents, in turn, should be joining together and fighting for themselves.

What follows should be considered a kind of challenge, a test case readers themselves can use to monitor the progress of foreign news coverage in the near future. Below I list a series of overlooked topics seriously in need of attention because they directly impact America and its security. I challenge my fellow foreign correspondents to report on them. And I ask the public to watch and see whether, after this book's publication, anyone has pursued the challenge. If not, I rest my case. If yes, there's hope yet.

■ As we've already touched on in some detail, Russian power is undergoing a serious resurgence. Russia appears to be successfully reconstituting the old Soviet sphere of influence. In the Soviet era, however, Russia's satellites were at least granted representation for their regions through the Supreme Soviet. Indeed many Politburo members, such as Shevardnadze of Georgia and Aliyev of Azerbaijan, originated from the "near-abroad" and fought for their region's interests. Now Russia effectively controls the economy of many

former satellites—*without offering them any representation.* Are we ready for such a new Russian empire,
and one governed on such terms? Shouldn't we be
learning more about the phenomenon? Why aren't we
doing so? As Radek Sikorski says in a recent London
Spectator article, "If in five years' time we again have
to increase our defence budgets to face a threat from a
reconstituted empire that, as usual, externalises its internal strains, this is the moment when the process
may become irreversible, and we will have ourselves
partly to blame."[5]

Russia's blatant meddling in the rigged and fraudulent 2004 Ukrainian presidential election should have
been a warning to us all. Yet much of the American
media arrived late on the story and provided little context, failing to identify the development as another example of revived Russian empire-building. In effect,
that meant the American public would largely ignore
the story, which suited the White House just fine.

When obviously important strategic or war zone
stories go unreported, the deafening silence usually
originates in Washington. The government doesn't want
too much scrutiny of its distant playing fields, and in
their commonplace laziness the news channels can generally be counted on to follow suit. Tease away at any
such neglected stories long enough, and Washington's
hidden interests will soon emerge. They don't always
coincide with the nation's interests; otherwise Washington would hardly mute the volume on them. So when I
ask why no one has examined a given topic, I include
any attendant media blackout as a separate topic in itself. Why the silence? Who benefits from it?

- Russia is now openly threatening such satellites as Armenia and Ukraine with embargos on fuel and other resources if they don't toe the line. When Armenia wanted to send a small contingent of fifty troops to serve with the Allies in Iraq, Russia successfully vetoed the idea by threatening to seal off the Armenian border, stopped trains from rolling and withheld trade including fuel until Armenia caved in. Outrageous? Of course. So why didn't the story get covered in the American media? Why no public protest from Washington? (Or, to take the question from the opposite perspective: Why did President Putin publicly support President Bush's presidential candidacy?)

- Could it be that Russia has successfully neutralized pressure from Washington by giving giant American oil companies major rights to extract oil from Siberia and the Bering Strait? How close are these corporations to the Bush White House, and do their interests coincide with the national interest? The answer might indeed be yes, in that we need the oil—but at what cost to our leverage abroad?

- Venezuela's Hugo Chavez openly boasts of his allegiance to Castro, and his contempt for U.S. policy. His goons regularly intimidate and kill people from the opposition. Venezuela ranks as one of the world's top oil exporters—in 2004 it was the world's fourth largest after Saudi Arabia, Russia, and Norway, and a prime furnisher to the American market. The Venezuelan news media often report that Chavez gives sanctuary to both Colombian guerillas and al Qaeda operatives. Let me repeat that: The leader of Venezuela gives sanctuary to al Qaeda. He also helps subsidize the Cuban economy with his oil revenue. Yet, beyond a few cautious murmurs of disapproval from the State Department, Chavez has gotten a free pass. Could it be because he has also given Texas-based oil giants such as Chevron-Texaco massive, lucrative contracts?

- In the weeks leading up to the American presidential election of 2004, the EU began preparing the ground to sell arms to China. On a highly public state visit to China, French president Jacques Chirac asked to have the existing EU embargo lifted on arms deals with China, in place since the Tienanmen massacre. The story got virtually no coverage stateside. Why not? Perhaps for the same reason that most other criticism of China never sees the light of day: many major American corporations that have invested billions of dollars in China (and made major outsourcing deals there) also own major news outlets such as NBC and the Fox News Channel.

- Nor has anyone reported that, over the years, China has operated in league with Pakistan against their mutual rival India to aid separatist fundamentalists in Indian Kashmir. China has also helped the Taliban in various ways: Ahmad Shah Massoud, who led resistance to the Taliban for years and was assassinated just before the U.S. invasion of Afghanistan, complained for years that Chinese Muslims were often captured fighting on the Taliban side. China and Pakistan had a secret deal to siphon off troublesome Islamists in China's repressed western Muslim provinces into Kashmir and Afghanistan. In return, China helped Pakistan develop its nuclear deterrent for years. In all the hubbub about Pakistan's export of nuclear know-how to

Libya, North Korea, and elsewhere, all of this went virtually unmentioned.

- Vladimir Putin caused a storm of protest in Eastern Europe in late October 2004 when he appeared on a call-in chat show in the Ukraine just before that country's presidential election. Putin strongly endorsed his preferred candidate, making it clear that affairs with Russia would go more smoothly if Ukrainians preferred his choice too. Considering that Russia can cut off oil and natural gas supplies to the Ukraine at will, many European observers accused Putin of trying to bully his colonies back into line. Again, though, the American news media let the incident pass with little comment.

- On the home front, the last-minute brouhaha about 370 tons of missing explosives from the Al Qaqaa weapons complex in Iraq has the strange, inconsistent quality of an even bigger underlying story struggling to stay dormant. Hard to tell what that story might be, but consider the following: in an October 27, 2004, story, the *Washington Times*'s Bill Gertz quoted Pentagon sources saying that Russian Special Forces, with Saddam's permission, had moved all Russian-made heavy ordnance from Iraq to Syria just before the American invasion. Pentagon sources claimed they'd only just received the information from two European intelligence services—just in time to rebut the Kerry camp's accusations of negligence. Sounds like late-breaking spin, right? Certainly, it seemed clear from videotapes taken at the time that U.S. soldiers had broken open one part of the complex, previously sealed by UN weapons inspectors. Ergo, the troops had opened the door to potential looting—another black eye for the White House's handling of the war.

But the Russian story may yet be true: Rumors had circulated for months in Iraq that Russians had also removed WMD before the war to Syria and Lebanon in precisely the same way. Speaking on deep background, in 2003 one Pentagon source told the New York-based veteran British journalist Anthony Haden Guest a similar tale, almost a full year before the U.S. presidential election: according to the source, WMD had been trucked into Syria by unknown elements a month before the U.S. invasion, and were now being kept in burial sites in Lebanon. Yet, no one would print Haden Guest's report in the American press, because his official source refused to be identified. (That Pentagon official, John A. Shaw, later went public on the Russians-at-Al Qaqaa controversy.)

Haden Guest had actually gone to Syria and Lebanon to confirm the story with Lebanese underground contacts who hated Syria; he finally published it in the November 2004 issue of British *Esquire*. If official U.S. sources knew about such shenanigans, why would they wait so long to go public with it? Then why did they go public about the Al Qaqaa arms site and leak to the *Washington Times*? Haden Guest has also asked why no one has launched an official probe into what he uncovered. Some in the Arab world believe that the Bush White House was waiting for reelection before "discovering" such information, in a bid to use it as a *casus belli* to move on Syria. U.S. intelligence had certainly watched heavy weapons and WMD sites in Iraq for months before invading; Russian Special Forces could hardly have removed such massive quantities of ordnance from known sites without anyone inside or outside Iraq noticing. Whether the evidence points to unimaginable U.S. blindness or some hidden strategy, it certainly suggests Russian treachery. Where, then, is the negative impact on Russian-American relations? And where are all the correspondents following in the footsteps of Haden Guest?

- The UN Oil-for-Food scandal has been making news for many months. As laid out by journalists working chiefly for pro-Republican news outlets such as Fox and the *National Review,* the UN allowed Saddam to extract many billions of dollars illegally from the supposedly UN-monitored humanitarian program, using the money to finance his regime. Saddam's strategy apparently involved getting kickbacks from international companies that sold Iraqi oil while supplying food and medicine to Saddam's Iraq. Most Iraqi locals knew, for example, that the shipments of oil out of Iraq via Kurdistan into Turkey, in trucks mostly driven by Kurds, all smuggled out extra oil illicitly in additionally fitted tanks. Kurds in both Iraq and Turkey benefited massively from the activity. Everyone knew, as surely did all American agents in the area, that the Oil-for-Food program was leaking from every orifice. No one has followed up on these anomalies. Why not?

- At first, the lists itemizing these companies suggested that most of them were French, Russian, or broadly Muslim in origin. Eventually, though, the *New York Times* revealed that a number of Texan companies also were involved. Various foreign countries and corporations have wondered angrily why no one probes this evidence of American involvement in the program.

Ten complex, nuanced, but highly important subjects of inquiry for my colleagues to ponder. Why has no one broached any of them? No doubt there are plenty of *ad hoc* reasons and excuses to be had in each case, but I can suggest one overarching cause: the disappearing foreign correspondent. These days, such intricate and deeply buried stories are unlikely to emerge into the public light unless some partisan political force wants them outed. And even those that do fade quickly unless someone with political clout manages to keep them in the public eye.

Once upon a time, respected correspondents possessed the supra-political leverage required to pursue such stories—and their employers, who had long invested in their stature, felt obliged to back them. Correspondents didn't need leaks or prods from power groups to go after a story (though such things never hurt); there was always enough money in the kitty and a boss sympathetic enough to endorse your efforts to find, develop, and finally nail a story for its own sake. What kind of a low have we plumbed when our foreign correspondents daily tiptoe over ground strewn with vital stories because most of us can't get them past our editors?

For all these reasons, the anodyne murmurs of the news anchors we visited in chapter six should offer us no solace. Peter Jennings, Tom Brokaw, and Dan Rather are all friends of mine. But as they have grown increasingly powerful in their profession, their less powerful colleagues have lost their ability to serve the public. Peter Jennings mourns the passing of the time when studio anchors and star reporters could be foreign correspondents first. But what did he do to try to stop it? Tom Brokaw plans to retire as anchor and use his fame and stature to do more long-form, investigative pieces. What was stopping him from sending his correspondents out to do that for the last fifteen years or so? It's no accident that the foreign correspondent's decline exactly parallels the industry's own. We will not revive one without reviving the other.

CHAPTER NINE

SOLUTIONS

If there were an easy way for today's news bosses to make money while providing well-made, in-depth, investigative hard news stories, someone would have thought of it by now. It's not as though the top anchors, and the other leading lights of our profession, actively prefer to dumb down their work. Virtually all of them believe, quite passionately, that the public remains woefully uninformed about crucial matters, and particularly about matters abroad. And most have given the subject a lot of thought. Yet no one has solved the problem; hence this book. When even those who benefit personally from the system tell you it needs fixing, without doing anything about it, it's impossible not to conclude that it's grievously flawed. The situation is so dire that simply complaining or equivocating will no longer suffice. It's time for practical solutions.

As I've argued in past chapters, it was not always thus. There were moments when America's insularity didn't matter as much; when Americans wanted to know more, and got what they wanted, as in the Cold War; or even when the news business told them what they didn't want to know and they listened, as in Vietnam. The success of *60 Minutes* showed us that hard news and profits could go in tandem. If so in the past, why not in the future? Perhaps the American scene has changed so thoroughly in recent years that there's no going back. Even the great unassailable bastion of *60 Minutes* makes its compromises. According to inside sources, *60 Minutes Wednesday* (formerly *60 Minutes II*) is under pressure from management to spur the ratings by popularizing and dumbing down its fare.

Is there no exit from the quandary? Does intelligent news always automatically mean fewer viewers? The industry bosses seem to think so, although there are plenty of journalistic voices at the top who still insist publicly that important foreign news, presented the right way, can pay for itself and more. Nevertheless, the industry groupthink persists—especially within the ranks of management, who argue from a defensive standpoint. For the bosses, it must be hard to resist the victim's posture, in which the journalists are the idealistic losers, and management are the hardheaded, cynical realists.

In fact, there's no rule that says intelligent news and profits work in inverse ratio to each other. Peter Jennings is one media figure who believes there is a market for quality foreign news—one that could be exploited by the first network to embrace that market.

"What I try to tell my bosses these days," Jennings says, "and I don't believe the Disney people believe this, is [that] we have got to stop trying to be all things to all people, because that's not the way the world turns any longer. What we should be is—and I often use *The Economist* as an example—a broadcast to which you turn every night simply to get some context. We should make our reputation as we made it in the first place."

As Jennings noted, the reputations of the networks for foreign reporting have shifted somewhat over the years. "CBS had a reputation for many, many years [for] foreign news," he notes—yet, he adds rather proudly, "I helped to take [that] away from you by our coverage, by our emphasis on foreign news." Still, Jennings concurs, you're only as good as your latest scoops: "It still lingers in the air, [the belief] that we do more foreign news, [but] it's not as deserved today as it used to be. So I would say to management, Why don't we try to get it back? Why don't we just say, you want to watch foreign news, watch ABC News?"

Realistically, though, the goal must go beyond simply offering more and better news from abroad. Only a revival of the infrastructure of bureaus and correspondents can truly restore the news business as the public service America desperately needs. It's a chicken-or-egg quandary: You can't improve the news without first expanding news-gathering capacity, which involves expenditure and a substantial hit to the bottom line.

Yet, as it happens, the technology exists to improve foreign news coverage *and* cut costs at the same time. Tom Bettag of *Nightline* argues that hand-held DVD recorders offer precisely this possibility—if management will seize it.

The challenge for the networks, Bettag says, was always whether to have "a big bureau, which is really expensive, or to put a ton of equipment on a plane and fly it into someplace and insure it, with air fares for a three- or probably four-man crew, which is incredibly expensive." Satellites, too, can be extremely costly. "[Networks] didn't want to go to Tokyo because the satellite costs are way higher than other people's," Bettag says. "But we have now moved into a world where you can have one reporter with a DVD camera who can go in for a month in some places and get the story. The technology has become such that that person can edit that story on a laptop, and email that story back to the States, less expensively than it takes to do a domestic story. You can already do it, but it will be much easier. And everybody who is saying we can't do it because it is too expensive, they're not looking at ways to [make] it cheaper. The organization that learns how to exploit that has a chance to do a huge jump on everything else."

If you build it they will come: It's an attractive theory. But who's going to invest the upfront as a loss leader and await the return? At present, no one has stepped forward to be the first. Among other things, there's no pressure from outside to do so—no forcible nudge to the conscience, no reminder of the networks' public responsibility.

All of this, of course, assumes that the news business should be a profit-making venture at all—another debate that has gone neglected too long. Many people point to the increasing popularity of National Public Radio as a promising model for alternative non-profit news broadcasting. Before 9/11, NPR had not quite 15 million listeners a day. That figure shot up to more than 19 million after the attacks, and by the spring of 2004 it had reached 22 million, an increase of 51 percent in the past four years. (By comparison, the top-rated network television evening news show, the *NBC Nightly News,* was down to an average of 11.4 million viewers a night in the first week of November 2004. ABC's *World News Tonight* had 9.6 million viewers, the *CBS Evening News* only 7.7 million.)

The increased popularity of public radio may demonstrate that many Americans are looking for more serious news. More and more, though, NPR does depends on public reactions, in the form of its ubiquitous on-air fund drives. My gut feeling on the issue is that any totally subsidized venture eventually grows insular and out of touch, falls out of synch with the real world. Indeed, our profession suffered in just that way during the Reagan era, when we continued to assume that the liberal yardstick on news still implicitly applied to everything. No, the correct perspective—one that keeps the profession on its toes—would require a news organization to make a modest profit, or at least to pay for itself. Yet our news industry's current addiction to the almighty dollar cannot survive much longer. The news business cannot serve the public while simultaneously acting as a mindless profit-center for corporate needs. And yet that is precisely what it has been trying, for far too long, to do.

There is one area, though, in which television should emphatically return to non-profit principles—the scourge of paid political advertising. Other countries, such as the United Kingdom, have a perfectly civilized solution to the problem: They allow free airtime to party political broadcasts. Just as corporations shouldn't be in the business of profiting from junk news, they should stay out of profiting from political ads. It's a murky, seedy gray area in which attack ads proliferate and civilized standards deteriorate with every election. Already, news-owning channels have entered the minefield of choosing which ads to run and which to curb or soften for public consumption. Paid political ads are generally defended on the grounds of free speech, but when the networks are cherry-picking ads for reasons of taste, the First Amendment argument doesn't hold up. After all, no one has yet broadcast anti-Bush ads showing pictures of dead Iraqi children. Why not, if it's a matter of total free speech? It isn't—it's about corporate profits, and the TV corporations should stop hiding behind the First Amendment because it could never protect their good-taste criteria from a serious constitutional challenge.

In the meantime, when it comes to the deteriorating judgment and practices of the networks, shareholders should put civic conscience before their pockets. Here's Don Hewitt on the subject of election-time TV costs:

> The role that television plays in politics? We're the masters of ceremonies of their political conventions. We participate in their debates. We take it upon ourselves to call their elections, and we make tons of money selling them time on television.
>
> I am sad to say I had a hand in that questionable practice. It all began with the 1960 television presidential debate between Richard Nixon and John F. Kennedy, which I was proud to say I produced and directed, [but] now in hindsight have second thoughts about. Because that was the night the politicians looked at television and said, *Those guys are the only way to run for office.* And we looked at them and said, *These guys are a bottomless pit of advertising dollars.* And from that moment on, the number one qualification to hold office in the world's greatest democracy is the ability to raise money for television time. Which virtually no candidate for public office can do without being in bed with, or at least in the pocket of, one or more special interests.
>
> [All of] which knocks into a cocked hat the founding fathers' notion that office holders in this wonderful new democracy would be freely elected, never dreaming that two hundred years hence an appliance called television would make that an impossibility. Think about this: In 1932 it cost the Democratic National Committee all of about 2.6 million dollars to elect Franklin Delano Roosevelt president of the United States. In today's dollars that's somewhere north of thirty million. Which is a helluva lot less than it costs in media buys alone to win just one seat in the United States Senate [today].
>
> With that stunning fact in mind, one thought has occurred to me to clean up the political mess: make it illegal for anyone doing business with the government to make

contributions to political candidates. I know that would bump up against the First Amendment, but I can't believe that the founding fathers had anything like that in mind when they devised the First Amendment.

So what to do? One thing I would do is rule out paid political advertising on television. Also a violation of the First Amendment? Probably. Maybe we could insist on a warning on paid political commercials like they put on cigarette packs: "Watching a paid political commercial is injurious to your health."

In politics, selling favors to people who want something from you is called fundraising. In business, it's called bribery.

If the news networks are supposed to be guardians of the public interest, how have we come to accept—or expect—so little of them? Are we doomed to be forever underinformed and blind to storm clouds gathering abroad (and at home), unable to anticipate attacks or even to monitor our own government's actions in our own defense? No doubt the cable news networks, talk radio commentators, and bloggers will gladly take up the slack as network news wanes in influence. But all those venues, as we've seen, ultimately offer opinion and comment at the expense of factual investigation.

Moreover, as Americans get their "news" from a host of competing, and often sensationalistic, sources, a national consensus becomes increasingly unattainable: People stop listening to opposing voices, the middle melts away, and empirical reality is replaced by spin. The old sensation of a country gathered together to watch the news, focused by a strong sense of shared trust in the news voice, may not come again. Perhaps we should merely bow our heads stoically and accept this as a function of unopposable market forces, as impervious to human influence as the weather. Our corporate bosses certainly believe we should. They own us. They believe junk news sells. As it is, the talent coming up through the ranks simply may not have any real notion of hard-news standards as they used to be. Raised on the entertainment-news of the 1990s, accustomed to corporate *diktat* as the ultimate arbiter of news choices, how can they possibly accrue the authority and worldwide experience the job used to require?

The news business might be the only business that routinely fails to deliver what it's supposed to and gets away with it—even profits from it. Detroit used to do that with cars, until Ralph Nader and Japanese competition came along in the 1970s. For decades, the Big Three auto makers had held American consumers in their thrall; with no serious competition in the domestic marketplace, car buyers couldn't imagine a higher standard than what Detroit offered. The result was that GM, Ford, and Chrysler grew complacent and sloppy—until Nader demonstrated that Detroit could deliver higher standards of safety if pushed, and the Japanese showed that Americans recognized better cars when they were made available.

It's an encouraging analogy, if not yet a perfect one. Americans are starting to realize that their news outlets don't serve their needs adequately. Whether they choose to supplement the nightly news with BBC or blogs or other alternatives—or replace it altogether—remains to be seen. Dan Rather notes that "for most people—not everybody, because you have to pay something to get cable, and not everybody in the country has cable—there is more international news on American television sets today than there has ever been. Examples: You can get a broadcast in French on my Manhattan Cable. Every night you get a French TV world roundup. You can get the BBC every night, ITN every night, plus at least two of the cable so-called all news networks. I say so-called because they are not all news, as you well know."

For a while, the 24-hour cable news channels promised to set a new standard, in which more time equaled more news. Inexorably, though, the same fast-profit exigencies subsumed their format too. Anyone accustomed to watching CNN abroad, or the BBC in England, cannot believe what those channels offer in the U.S. market: the shorter bulletin items, the newsmagazine-like trend segments on America. They manifestly assume that American tastes simply cannot be raised; easy revenue with cheaper outlay and less hard news pays off too easily. Nobody has ever gone broke underestimating the American public, right? It's as if the Japanese had decided that they too could prosper by feeding the preconditioned American market the standard-issue flashy gas-guzzling junk cars of old. The Japanese, though, did precisely the opposite. They sensed a market gap—for quality product at an affordable price—and they seized the opportunity.

The same market gap exists in news, as more and more Americans are coming to realize. As yet, though, the industry has failed to respond; it remains wedded to the needs of the corporation, orders from above, rather than to the public's demands.

What to do? If the existing news structures are to be saved and improved rather than replaced by a warren of fragmentary news sources, then the public's voice must be amplified to reach the ears of corporate news-owning bosses. No amount of Pew studies or damning stats will shake the owners' addiction to the formula that cheap news equals healthier profits. Certainly the pressure must come from the American public. As it stands, however, the public's demands get dissipated in the complex decentralized structure of channel ownership.

Local television stations are the real profit centers. The networks that supply programs to affiliate stations have slim profit margins, but the owners of the stations make bags of money broadcasting on the nation's free airwaves. Which explains why the local stations have always resisted suggestions to expand the network news broadcasts, or move them into the evening hours, which are traditionally filled with the most popular and profitable entertainment shows. How to deliver the public's voice both broadly enough to reach all those affiliated power centers and loudly enough to reach the top echelons at corporate headquarters? Some suggest that pressure be focused where it can most easily: on the Federal Communication Commission (FCC) in Washington. Walter Cronkite says he doesn't understand "why local groups don't get together and hold the local stations' feet to the fire by threatening their licenses."

The trouble, as we've seen, is that the FCC is a toothless tiger. It has rarely leaned on the networks to perform better,[1] and it certainly won't change its stripes now that FCC rules have changed to allow the networks to own more local stations in more markets. One can scarcely accuse the FCC of being uniquely feckless. As Ralph Nader shows in his recent book *The Good Fight,* corporate power and money dominate Washington so totally that most watchdog agencies actively strive as a matter of policy to facilitate business interests first. The FCC is no different: "deregulation of the cable industry has sent cable rates higher as giant mergers leave viewers with less and less competition and choice of quality viewing." As Nader notes, "In 1996, the FCC gave away what then-presidential candidate Bob Dole estimated to be a $75 billion asset of the American people—the digital spectrum—to the broadcast industry."[2]

For the public to have an impact, it has to be roused and its anger focused; this can be done most effectively when a pressure group steps in to amplify the public demands, as Nader did against Detroit. I hope that this book will contribute to the cause, but for Americans to take on the corporate power elites in charge of networks and news channels, the pressure must build and remain continuous. Consumers successfully apply such pressure on the media all the time for other reasons: the NAACP, the Anti-Defamation League, any number of minority rights organizations, and a lot of conservative groups all monitor media output, often complaining about media bias. Why not a lobby that monitors and insists on news quality and quantity? If it can be done with cars or beef or the environment, why not with news?

Walter Cronkite has given this challenge serious contemplation. Taking a dim view of the industry's current condition, he believes it's time for just such a vehicle:

> What we need to do is to [call on] the journalistic fraternity to put more pressure on the commercial interests, with a united front. If you could put together a society for the purpose of continually bringing public attention to the failures of the broadcasters, they [might] be inclined—embarrassed enough—to give us more time and to be sure that we are financed adequately. That whole business of cutting down a lot of bureaus overseas—we can prove where that caused trouble. I think the first Gulf War, the Iraqi invasion of Kuwait, could have been foreseen if we had somebody covering the Middle East carefully enough and understanding what Saddam Hussein was up to, what he was moving toward. Putting the diplomatic pressure on him via the press, we might have avoided the First Gulf War, and almost certainly the second one, with the proper coverage.

What can we do as journalists? That, I would suggest, could be a matter of awakening the journalists' fraternity. The journalism schools, the good ones—Columbia, Northwest, and so forth—should let their deans put what public pressure they can on top working journalists. And those who are constantly pointing out our faults, our problems, need somehow to organize so that they become a lobbying group. Let them fund a lobby in Washington—it needs to be in the nation's capital, simply to give it the cache of a lobbying organization. Label it as such, that this body will constantly put the pressure on the commercial interests, the publishers and the broadcasters. . . .

If [such an] organization could be inspired to work more diligently in calling attention to the failures of the media, calling attention to the public, it would put pressure on the ownership to mend its ways.

A number of organizations already cover some of this territory, but none do so as thoroughly as Cronkite suggests. The National Press Club in Washington, D.C., for example, provides one of the most prestigious venues for newsmakers—from financier George Soros to Afghanistan's Hamid Karzai to Pakistan's Pervez Musharraf—to address the American press directly. Most journalists belong to any number of such foundations, political or otherwise. But so far no *ad hoc* body has taken on the specific task of shaming news owners into giving more and better news, period. More and better about Muslims, yes; more and better about Hispanics, gays, prisoners, fur-bearing animals, the deaf, blind, or handicapped, yes. Their advocacy groups have all done their share to improve or sensitize news media awareness to their cause. And they often do so by shaming egregiously insensitive, one-sided, or ill-informed news reports. But no one has, yet, conceived the notion of civil disobedience for all-round better news.

Ideally, such an organization would be more than just a well-intentioned trade guild; it would be a desperately needed service to the American people. For, in my view, the monomaniacal greed of the news organizations has kept Americans dangerously underinformed and put us in peril as surely as badly made cars once did—even as Americans have forgotten to expect anything more. As Cronkite points out, the networks can be spurred to react quickly and decisively when they're made to feel the heat—as they did after Janet Jackson's infamous "wardrobe malfunction" at the 2004 Super Bowl:

> Look at the reaction at CBS when this ridiculous episode occurred. . . . Look at how quickly CBS responded to that. So there is a sensitivity there. They *can* be touched, if it is a tough enough organization that the newspapers and the broadcasters would be forced to promise some allegiance to that organization as an inspirational group.

Such a group should be open to members of every corner of American journalism; given how thoroughly their livelihood has been compromised, however, we foreign correspondents should be first in line to join. In thirty-four years of covering foreign news on television, my most frustrating moments were spent at the mercy of uninformed network executives, who were content to deep-six important stories without any fear of being exposed for their ignorance. If their bad decisions were purely a matter of bias, of course—left wing, right wing, antiminority—they would have had an inner voice warning them to think again, or at least an awareness of the potential public outcry that would inevitably follow. A defining goal of this new organization would be to encourage the network executives to think twice about every such questionable decision they make—to stand as a sentinel of quality for the industry as a whole. The correspondents could be supported in the lobby by authoritative veterans such as Cronkite or Marvin Kalb, many of whom now work in academia or foundations. No currently employed reporters could be expected to blow the whistle on one of the networks without fear of being fired and survive—unless a phalanx of public figures were there to stand beside them. And the public itself should have a hand in the proceedings—the more the better. After all, when the news business fails at its most fundamental task—as we saw on 9/11—it's the American people who pay the price.

What, in concrete terms, could such a pressure group ask for from news channels? That raises a broader question: How do we define quality in news?

We can start with one simple equation: In the news business, you can't improve quality without increasing quantity. As I've said, the limitations of the current news format have forced producers to run triage: With no more than seventeen minutes or so each evening to cover the news, context, geography, history, investigation and explanation all go by the wayside. And quantity requires more funding, which in turn requires more revenue.

In the survey I conducted among my peers about possible solutions, one idea kept recurring: the hour-long news broadcast. To many Americans long accustomed to dreary presentation of dissociated news disasters and human interest fluff items from abroad, this may sound like a guaranteed disaster.

A whole hour, you may ask? Well, yes, and it's way past due, at least according to a consensus of my peers. For those of us within the industry, it's a tangible and practical goal; for the rest of the country it would mean a sea-change in the quality of the reporting they watch every night.

Walter Cronkite suggests two network news broadcasts every evening: the regular evening news at 6.30 P.M. as a head-line service, and an hour-long instant documentary at 9 P.M. on the day's top story. To him, this formula is the only way "to fully discharge our responsibilities, which are very heavy":

> It should be obvious that we do not have enough time for daily reporting to do the job that needs to be done. Sixteen or seventeen minutes of copy-that's ridiculous when we have a nation that's as complicated as ours, and a world that is getting more complicated every moment as we sit here not doing anything about uncomplicating it. . . .
>
> I always thought we ought to have that eleven o'clock spot, or ten o'clock preferably, for an hour. Obviously, that never came about, and the problem as we have always known has been the affiliates. There are not going to give us part of [prime] time—that is, their time to make money. We have now broken through that shibboleth and have these magazine shows on: One hour, three nights a week. What do we do with them? Sex, crime, and that's about it.
>
> What we should be doing is taking those periods of time and doing instant documentaries. We would have the capa-bility of doing it, we know how to do it in the news depart-ment. Some may say it's impossible. It's not impossible, you damn well know. We work a little bit ahead to get some of the background of stories we know are going to break, then the day they break, we go and get the last statements. That way you get the headlines at six-thirty, [and] at nine o'clock you get the full substance of the story.

As Cronkite notes, this would very much follow the model set by PBS with *The NewsHour with Jim Lehrer* (the current iteration of the old *McNeil-Lehrer Report*)—one of the few shows on television that offers truly in-depth news coverage.

Dan Rather has been talking about a one-hour prime-time evening news for more than twenty-five years. He raised the question with CBS management when he took over from Cronkite as anchor of the evening news in 1981; at one time a few years later, the affiliate stations flirted with approving it before backing off. The idea surfaced again at the time of the first Gulf War, but again it was shot down. Even within the last year, Rather told me, he brought the subject up with management again. What was the response, I asked?

"They say, with a smile, 'It's a wonderful idea and I would love to do it, but Dan, it's not worth talking about because it's not going to happen.' That's a paraphrase, but a pretty accurate paraphrase."

Rather has never given up the dream of an hour show—which, in his view, "would make all the difference in the world." He sees the recent multiplication of the number of local stations owned by the networks as a new opportunity.

"Remember," Rather says, "for a long time the networks were limited in the number of stations that they could own and operate. The limit at one time was six stations. There is still a limit, but now . . . it is not unusual for a network to own fifteen, sixteen, seventeen stations."[3] To Rather, "the best hope of getting an hour-seven-days-across-the-board news program" would be for one of those networks with fifteen to seventeen stations to say, "We are going to do it on our stations. Any other affiliates that want to take it can do so." As Rather says, a daily hour-long broadcast would be a crucial step in "reestablishing our commitment to strong, aggressive, bold, overseas coverage, as well as some other kinds of coverage—we don't cover government as well as we once did, either."

Thus far, as Rather concedes, such an idea "has only been talked about as far as I know in the vaguest sort of way." And when it has, "the answer is, Well, that would present a lot of complications. I have no doubt that it would. But if—and this is my story, this is my song—if you want to lead, in both public service and, I think, in brand name and bottom line [terms], you have to make a bold move. That's what leadership is about. So somebody—I'm hoping it's us—will say, You know what, it *may* cost us something in the beginning, but we will expand the evening news to an hour, either in its present time form or, as crazy Rather wants, at ten o'clock at night.

"I'm convinced it would not only be a good public service, but after a lifetime in commercial radio and television, I'm convinced that it would also be good business."

With Rather's departure, it remains to be seen whether someone else in a position of power will feel the same way.

Tom Brokaw, the other departing lion of the evening-news world, shares Rather's strong feelings. In fact, he told me that if NBC had agreed to expand the evening news to an hour, he probably would have changed his decision to step down from the anchor chair. It's one of the chief frustrations of his career:

> It should be longer. The evening news should be an hour. It makes me crazy. If they had said to me a year ago, *Hey, listen, if we make the evening news an hour would you stay?* I probably would have stayed. I am not sure how long, but I probably would have stayed at least another year or two. Because it has always been my dream that we need a larger screen on which to play out there, and I happen to believe that there is an unrealized appetite for it. It does not mean that if I were to go to the main street of Hayes, Nebraska,

and say, 'How about an evening news that is an hour long?' [people would welcome it immediately]. But I think if you did it in the correct fashion, they would come. Like a field of dreams.

I asked him what time slot he would prefer for his ideal news hour.

Well, that's the conundrum. I would put it on at seven. Seven to eight is owned by the owned stations. Most of the stations are now owned by the networks. It is a huge revenue producer for them. The FCC decreed that the local stations control access to prime time, so they can do programming of local interest. Which means *Jeopardy, Who Wants to Be a Millionaire?* or whatever else is there. That's a frustration for me.

And one of the things that happens is that from time to time they will do my show for an hour—but it's generally around a big event. We did an hour for a couple of weeks after 9/11. The last time we did an hour around a single event, I believe, was the night they captured the snipers in the Washington, D.C., area. From time to time, I'll say there will be a huge news day of some kind, and I'll say let's go ask if we can get an hour. They poll the stations, and they say, *Yeah, we'll give you the extra half hour tonight.* It almost always works out.

The problem of asking longstanding news professionals for solutions is that, though they are best qualified to know the business from within, they are also deeply embedded in its predictable ways. Yet, it's clear that many of them have been trying—from a mixture of idealism and despair—to think outside the box. The one-hour news idea has apparently so sparked the imagination of our news leaders that they've thought it through down to the nitty-gritty of affiliate relations—of how to effect such a massive structural change while using the building blocks that exist. It bears repeating: It's a sad statement on the state of our news business that so many of the networks' top anchors and veteran professionals have virtually begged their networks for improvements like an hour news show—have even mapped out concrete solutions—yet been rebuffed time after time. It certainly gives me pause: If the combined force of their demands has produced no effective change, and if they haven't come up with a creative way to make it happen, one has to wonder too whether their solutions would work in practice.

Perhaps Americans, particularly younger Americans, have become too fluff-happy, too incapable of concerted attention, for an nightly hour-long news shows to take hold. Perhaps it would be asking for too much too late. Can a young demographic that tunes to comedian Jon Stewart's *The Daily Show* for its news ever come around to extended segments full of context presided over by veteran anchors? On the other hand, these are the last voices that carry the continuity from the old days of high standards into the present. Certainly no younger-skewed cable channels such as VH1 or MTV have even attempted a regular news show. They offer no solutions or alternative sense of duty. On balance, adding up the accumulated years of experience embodied in these news business professionals, you have to conclude that their unified wisdom stands for a good deal more than the usual groupthink. If they're better at thinking out loud than acting radically for change, I put it down, at least in part, to somewhat outdated notions of loyalty to employer and brand. Still, as they all inch closer to retirement, they may yet feel able to join the fight for change—especially if a truly powerful pressure group gets off the ground.

What would a news hour look like, assuming it goes beyond a slavish extension of what exists (or a pure copy of
PBS's nightly broadcast)? Tom Brokaw says he "could do the
construct in the next thirty seconds on the back of this napkin
for an hour show that I think would hold up every night":

> It would start with the way we start right now. And then we
> would take the model of what we call "In Depth." I get
> teased about that, because it is more of a marketing device,
> but I would really make it the big story of the day—you
> know, the significant sidebar.
>
> I would find a component for opinion. A component for
> what I call consumer news. We have become a raging con-
> sumer society; the competition for your buck every day is
> huge . . . [especially] for parents. So I'd find time for that.
> And I would have an opinion thing. The bloggers—that's a
> whole new world out there, [and] we are behind the curve
> on it. . . . There is a huge range of material out there. Med-
> ical bloggers, sports bloggers. It's an astonishing universe.
> In fact, I don't think anybody knows how big it really is. You
> may even want to try some kind of an interactive compo-
> nent, where you get letters, and they come interactively to
> the broadcast. I could be there saying, *This is what bloggers
> .com is saying tonight.* You can determine the integrity or
> credibility of them on a reasonably quick basis, and that be-
> comes some part of the opinion.
>
> [Between] opinion [and] the interactive component,
> that's pretty close to an hour right there. And then you come
> to the end of it and you do what I call a headline service—
> bang, bang, bang, to get you back up to date, and here's a
> calendar for the next day, what to expect.

I asked Brokaw if he truly would have stayed on as anchor if
NBC had given him an hour evening news show.

"Yeah, I would have," he responded. "It would have been hard to walk away from that, especially in these times. Part of the reason that I am walking away is that I am frustrated by the compression. I am going to go do documentaries and longer form stuff, going to write books. But mostly what I like to do at this stage of my life is to spend more time thinking about fewer subjects in greater detail. I mean, it's as simple as that."

I did not have to ask Andy Rooney what he thought about the hour evening news show. By coincidence, he had already aired the idea on *60 Minutes,* the evening before I was scheduled to interview him. And of course he did it in his in his own fashion—as an open letter to Sumner Redstone, the chairman of the board of Viacom, the company that owns CBS. He began by stating that the incident of the questionable documents used by Dan Rather on *60 Minutes* had hurt the credibility of CBS News, and then made his suggestion:

> How about this for reestablishing the credibility of CBS News? Turn our *Evening News with Dan Rather* into a one-hour broadcast, seven nights a week. Provide it as a public service in exchange for the license that CBS has to make hundreds of millions of dollars from the entertainment shows that Les Moonves puts on.
>
> The American public gets most of its news from television, and it doesn't get enough. The *Evening News* is twenty minutes long—nowhere near enough to tell Americans what's going on in their country, let alone anywhere else. One of the reasons America is hated around the world is because we're ignorant of everyone else's problems, and that's partly our fault. Television provides too little foreign news. So send a bunch of CBS reporters to other countries, too, so we give viewers an idea of what's happening somewhere other than here. If CBS News was on the air every night for an hour, it might make people forget this mistake.[4]

So we have the first steps of a road map on how to improve news: Create a pressure group, and begin by lobbying for hour-long broadcasts. Such broadcasts would also imply a demand that foreign bureaus be reopened, staffed with a respectable number of correspondents. With handheld DVD and laptop editing technology available, the costs need not be what they were in the past. And, since the grand old men of the business weren't able to convince their networks to hold back chunks of their salary to the networks to fund the reopening of bureaus, here's an alternative. Let them contribute to the pressure group—and participate in drawing up its manifesto and mission statement.

Throughout this book, I have tried to give concrete instances of bad judgments by news executives; where relevant, I have mentioned their names. The trouble is that nobody knows the names of most of the nay-saying news executives—and the effect doesn't compare to outing movie stars or public figures. But the pressure group's first job should be to out such people and their decisions. It should run a weekly register of egregious news shortfalls, and wherever possible attach the names of the culprits who should be held accountable.

Another concrete requirement for such an organization should be that it start its own publication and web site, to shine a continuous light on the daily decision-making practices of the news custodians. Just as I did in Chapter 8, the lobby should use these venues to publish a running list of unreported topics, demanding an explanation for why the topics remain undercovered. Also featured could be comparative lists of how the media in other countries reported stories differently from ours, or showed us up in reporting what we didn't. This would provide a forum for scrutinizing omissions or biased reporting, on laziness or insufficient resources. And there are still more potential functions for such a lobby, from exposing exactly how little or how much news shows spend on coverage—information that should be in the public domain anyway, since all the relevant corporations are publicly owned—to naming an all-round Year's Best and Year's Worst award, a la Time's Person of the Year, for outstanding achievement (or lack thereof) in improving news coverage. Can you imagine the odium of being publicly vilified by the Walter Cronkites of the world, in a National Correspondents' Dinner-style award ceremony broadcast on C-Span?

As I enter my retirement in 2005, I personally look forward to beating the drum on this enterprise—and on the broader struggle of expanding and improving news coverage. This book is certainly not an end in itself, but I hope it will be the beginning of a rising tide of consciousness that must, for all our sakes, bear concrete results. Most important, though, I invite everyone who cares about the world, and their country's place within it, to stand with me in challenging the corporate news owners to improve their standards. America, demand more and better news from those responsible for providing it. It might save all our lives.

NOTES

Chapter 1   The News Gap

1. ABC *World News Tonight,* June 6, 2002.
2. Peter L. Bergen, *Holy War, Inc.* (New York: Free Press, 2001; Touchstone, 2002).
3. Quoted by Howard Kurtz, *Washington Post,* June 10, 2002.
4. February 2003, poll data from the Pew Research Center for the People and the Press, quoted in *The State of the News Media 2004,* by the Project for Excellence in Journalism.
5. Bernard Goldberg, *Bias* (Washington, DC: Regnery, 2002).
6. David Javerbaum, on the *Leonard Lopate Show,* October 20, 2004.
7. "Missed Signals," *American Journalism Review,* August/September 2004.
8. Vaughn Ververs, "Blame the Messenger," *National Journal,* August 6, 2004.

Chapter 2   Wartime Duties: What Is at Stake, and What Is Our Role?

1. Interview with Hamid Mir, editor of the Pakistani newspaper *Dawn, CBS Evening News,* November 11, 2001.
2. Strobe Talbott, The Russia Hand: A Memoir of Presidential Diplomacy (New York: Random House, 2002).
3. A CBS News producer who prefers to remain anonymous recalls walking through the rubble of the factory two days after the missile strike, and writing an on-camera piece in which the

correspondent picked up bottles from the debris and read their labels. They appeared to be animal antibiotics. The *CBS Evening News* producers in New York forbade the team in Sudan to air it, and a new on-camera had to be done in which there was no implied criticism of the attack. The field producer who told me this said: "This felt like the beginning of the censorship we had always said did not exist. It now does; often it is tacit."

4. Fred Friendly was a towering figure in the history of broadcast news who came to stand for integrity in journalism. In the 1950s, he and legendary newsman Edward R. Murrow created for CBS News the program *See It Now,* the most critically-acclaimed television series of its time. Their 1954 broadcast on Senator Joseph McCarthy was widely credited with breaking the senator's grip on the country in that paranoid era. After fifteen years producing the finest programs in television news, Friendly was named president of CBS News in 1964. He resigned in 1966 after the network pre-empted congressional hearings on Vietnam to air reruns of *I Love Lucy.* Friendly joined the Ford Foundation, where he was one of the driving forces behind the creation of public television, and Columbia University, where he inspired a generation of journalists.

5. Michael Parks, "The Future of Foreign Coverage," *Columbia Journalism Review,* January/February 2002.

6. Ibid.

Chapter 3   How We Got Here

1. *Reporting World War II, Part One: American Journalism, 1938–1944* (New York: Library of America, 1995), p. 174.

2. Sanford Socolow, former CBS News vice president and executive producer of the *CBS Evening News,* says the CBS management used to hide the fact that news made money, in order to claim it was presenting the news as a public service. When I interviewed him for this book, he explained: "Ernie [Ernest] Leiser (a former CBS News executive, now deceased) told me that all the stuff about news being a loss leader was bullshit. News always made

money. The network could claim it was a money loser by the way they set up the bookkeeping. Here's how they did the accounting: The edit machines and editors *60 Minutes* used, for example, were owned by a unit called CBS Operations that charged *60 Minutes* an exorbitant price to use the machines and editors. It was probably legal, but it was a device to hide the profits. When Fred Friendly took over [as president of CBS News] he tried to put out the stuff for bids. The corporation put an immediate stop to that.

"In 1975 or '76, *60 Minutes* became number one for the first time. It made so much money that, short of doing something illegal or unethical, they couldn't hide it anymore. They wanted to say that they paid this tithe for the public weal. This was the obligation they owed the public. When I was a vice president briefly I got a chance to look at the phony bookkeeping. They tried to take the *60 Minutes* income and attribute it to the network. so it would not appear on the CBS News books. That didn't work."

3. *CBS News Standards,* edition of April 14, 1976, p. ii.

4. The American assault on Falluja in November, 2004, was an exception: American correspondents were embedded with the Marines and Army and were close to the action, but of course could only see one side of the battle. It was dangerous work, and at the time of this writing a number of my television news colleagues were refusing to go to Iraq—a disturbing development.

5. In the same interview, Socolow recalls: "When Tisch decided to make his famous tour of the CBS European bureaus, a friend of mine who is also a friend of Tisch, told me, 'You must be out of your fucking minds. You are going to let him wander around the world? You guys will never recover from this!' "

6. Various industry sources say it's difficult to quantify Disney's losses, since the recession was already in swing, which would have affected retail spending, theme park attendance and hotel revenues. Disney was also forced to postpone the release of the film *Collateral Damage* in the wake of 9/11. However, analysts speculate Disney may not have suffered as much as the others because the retail sector weathered the post-9/11 dip, leaving

film attendance relatively unaffected. GE sources say their company lost a combined total of $600 million: $400 million from re-insurance of World Trade Center properties, and $100 million each for NBC and GE's aircraft engines unit, which sold fewer spare parts and provided fewer maintenance services because of the reduction in flights. Jessica Reif Cohen of Merrill Lynch says that the CBS division of Viacom received damage recovery of $40 million post-9/11.

7. From *The State of the Media 2004:* "In November 1980, the year CNN was launched, 75 percent of television sets in use were tuned to one of the three nightly network newscasts each night during the dinner hour. In 2003, it was a 40 percent share. Of all television homes, 20.6 percent were tuned to the nightly news in November 2003, a drop of 44 percent from 1980, when the networks' nightly news broadcasts had a combined 37 rating. Yet, much of this decline did not come with the advent of cable, between 1980 and 1990. The drop in audience has been even steeper in the last 10 years, as the number of cable outlets has proliferated, than in the previous 13 years."

8. After the seizure of the American Embassy in 1979, the Iranians painstakingly pieced together many of the classified documents which had been shredded while the embassy was besieged, and published them in volumes called *The Documents from the Spy Nest.* They included memos to the State Department from the ambassador and other embassy officials correctly warning of the problems in the country, of what might happen and what an eruption of unrest could mean. Clearly, those in authority in Washington paid no more heed to the warnings than my bosses at CBS News.

Chapter 4   The Culture of Spin

1. *Washington Post,* October 5, 2004.

2. *Wall Street Journal,* Op-Ed, September 17, 2004, "Kremlin Democracy"

3. Peter Lance, *Cover Up: What the Government Is Still Hiding about the War on Terror* (New York: ReganBooks, 2004).

4. *Cover Up,* p. 227; Paul Thompson and the Center for Cooperative Research, *The Terror Timeline* (New York: ReganBooks, 2004), p. 307.

5. Early in the second Gulf War, General Tommy Franks said at a press briefing, "We don't do body counts." The website www.Iraqbodycount.net, collating data from reports in the media, estimated on November 9, 2004, that approximately 15,000 Iraqi civilians had died as a result of the military intervention in Iraq. A study published in the British medical journal *The Lancet* on October 29, 2004, using data gathered on the ground in Iraq and a standard epidemiological extrapolation methodology, estimated there were 100,000 deaths. Given the relative size of the two countries, that would be the equivalent of roughly 1.2 million American deaths.

6. *The Economist,* December 16, 2003, and also reported elsewhere.

7. *Washington Post,* July 4, 2004.

8. Thompson, *The Terror Timeline,* p. 306.

Chapter 5   What the Rest of the World Sees

1. Garrick Utley, *You Should Have Been Here Yesterday* (New York: Public Affairs, 2000), p. 203.

2. Most Americans may not be aware of it, but the same process has occurred in Italy in the last few years. There it was not the state *per se* that took over the media, but one man, Prime Minister Silvio Berlusconi. As head of the government, he already ran state-owned RAI television. Only in the old days, the political parties that used to make up the governing coalitions, shared between them the control of the different RAI channels. Berlusconi did away with the old arrangement and now virtually dictates what runs on RAI. What's more, he has used his influence and personal fortune to buy leading newspapers and build an empire of private television channels that feed the

public a diet of his right-wing views and trashy game and girlie shows.

3. For a while, after the collapse of the Soviet Union, the state loosened its grip on the Russian media. Sure, newspapers still depended on government supplies of newsprint and other subsidies and the state controlled the national television network, but a freer flow of information did become possible. Commercial television and independent newspapers began to tell the real story of the Russian army's bloody campaign to crush the rebellion in Chechnya. But after Vladimir Putin was elected president, things began to change. He cut down to size the powerful and immensely wealthy "oligarchs" who controlled huge chunks of the economy and large parts of the media. Above all, he reasserted tight government control over television—the main means of propaganda in a vast country where few people can still afford a daily newspaper. Even television news magazines and talk programs, which had briefly flourished in the 1990s, were curbed.

Chapter 6   Voices Inside the Industry

1. On January 31, 2001, a bipartisan panel—led by former U.S. senators Warren B. Rudman and Gary Hart, and including high-ranking military and former cabinet secretaries—called for the creation of a cabinet-level Homeland Security Agency to assume responsibility for defending the United States against the increasing likelihood of terrorist attacks in the country. Their report warned bluntly that terrorists would probably attack the United States with nuclear, chemical, or biological weapons at some point within the next twenty-five years.

2. "Public diplomacy" is the term used by the State Department to describe programs to inform and influence public opinion in other countries—that is, the effort to "win hearts and minds." Faced with the rise of anti-Americanism, especially in the Arab world, the government has tried Madison Avenue techniques to "tell the story" of the United States better, and to promote

"Brand USA." Yet many doubt the effectiveness of such efforts, since U.S. foreign policy, rather than bad PR, is most often cited as the reason for anti-U.S. sentiment.

3. The takeovers in the mid-1980s of ABC by Capital Cities, NBC by General Electric, and CBS by Larry Tisch's Loews Corporation.

4. CBS, like the other networks, has a contractual arrangement with its affiliate stations to carry the network's programs.

5. In 1976, ABC hired Barbara Walters from NBC as a co-anchor for their prime news time at a record-breaking one million dollars a year.

Chapter 7   History and Geography: What We Don't Know Can Kill Us

1. Djibouti, a former French colony at the mouth of the Red Sea, provides strategic leverage over Sudan, Eretria, Somalia, and Yemen. The United States now uses it as a military base in the war against terror. Russia and Greece, as fellow orthodox Christian lands, helped Serbia flout UN embargoes. Indeed, former Serb leader Slobodan Milosevic, now on trial for crimes against humanity, proposed that Greece and Serbia form a confederation in December 1994. See Takis Michas, *Unholy Alliance* (College Station, TX: Texas A&M University Press, 2002), p. 106.

2. Chalmers Johnson, "The Arithmetic of American Military Bases Abroad," History News Network (www.hnn.com), January 19, 2004.

3. Paul Klebinov, *Godfather of the Kremlin: Boris Berezovsky and the Looting of Russia* (New York: Harcourt, 2000).

4. Ibid., p. 303.

5. *Barbara Bush: A Memoir* (New York: Simon & Schuster, 1994).

6. John Cassidy, "Beneath the Sand," *New Yorker,* July 14, 2003.

7. Niall Ferguson, *Colossus: The Price of America's Empire* (New York: Penguin, 2004).

Chapter 8   Where Have They Gone, the Great Foreign Correspondents?

1. Bill Kotovsky and Timonthy Carlson, *Embedded: The Media at War In Iraq—An Oral History* (Lyons Press, 2003).

2. By contrast, Maceda says, the going rate for an Iraqi doctor on the kidnapping market is $100,000.

3. Charles Collingwood (1917–1985), one of the "Murrow Boys," the correspondents recruited for CBS News by Edward R. Murrow in World War II, who went on to become the stars of postwar broadcast news.

4. Seymour Hersh, *Chain of Command: The Road from 9/11 to Abu Ghraib* (New York: HarperCollins, 2004).

5. Radek Sikorski, "Yearning to Breathe Free," London *Spectator,* November 6, 2004. Sikorski had this to say about Russian manipulation of the recent national elections in Ukraine:

> The instances of cheating are just too numerous to allow a charitable explanation. Famously, the main challenger, Viktor Yushchenko, fell mysteriously ill the day after he ate supper with the country's intelligence chief and now looks 20 years older, his face twisted and swollen as if he'd been burned by napalm. Opposition rallies have been disrupted with electricity cuts or prevented from happening at all by arbitrary cancellations of rented facilities or of scheduled train and bus services. Government- and Russian-owned media pump blatantly biased propaganda devoting, according to independent observers, about 80 per cent of the time to promoting the Prime Minister, Viktor Yanukovych. The only opposition-inclined TV station, Channel 5, had its license suspended just a few days before the first round of voting last weekend. Radio and print journalists are routinely threatened; and this is no joke in a country in which nosy journalists are apt to disappear without trace.
>
> Russia has intervened forcefully on behalf of its man, Yanukovych. To welcome President Putin in Kiev for an unprecedented three days just before the poll, Kiev's military parade to mark the city's liberation from Nazi rule was brought

forward a week. Russian government TV's idea of a pre-election debate was to invite a Yanukovych supporter from Russia and a Yanukovych supporter from Ukraine. Russian PR agencies are advising Yanukovych, and thousands of voters received a 'Letter from Russia' which warned that an opposition victory would mean higher energy prices.

Chapter 9   Solutions

1. There was one instance in the mid-1970s when the FCC put pressure on the networks to hire more women and ethnic minorities. Networks were obliged to submit annual lists of female and minority hires, and officials at CBS were told that their bonuses would be affected by their hiring statistics. That era did not last.

2. Ralph Nader, *The Good Fight: Declare Your Independence and Close the Democraphy Gap* (New York: ReganBooks, 2004), p. 31.

3. There are two kinds of network television stations: those that are owned and operated by a network, and the "affiliates," which are owned by other entities but have a contractual arrangement with a network to carry its programs.

4. *60 Minutes,* October 3, 2004.

INDEX

L

M

N